It's All In the Way You Think

Jack Smith Stout

ISBN 0-7414-3176-9

Published by:

INFINITY PUBLISHING.COM

1094 New DeHaven Street, Suite 100
West Conshohocken, PA 19428-2713
Info@buybooksontheweb.com
www.buybooksontheweb.com
Toll-free (877) BUY BOOK
Local Phone (610) 941-9999
Fax (610) 941-9959

Printed in the United States of America

Printed on Recycled Paper

Published June 2006

CONTENTS

SECTION TWO: SOLUTIONS

SECTION THREE: CHANGE

PREFACE

This book is a product of over twenty-five years experience conducting what could broadly be called cognitive therapy groups, or what I have come to call Event Evaluation Therapy. Sometimes I use "therapy" and "training" interchangeably. All of the headings are actual topics that have been discussed in group sessions, many of which are the result of questions and suggestions from group participants. Thus, the topics (especially in the "applications" section) are wide ranging. For the most part group members have been inmates (both male and female) in correctional institutions and clients residing in a homeless shelter.

It is important for the reader to understand that, while I have written with inmates, former inmates, and homeless shelter residents in mind, it is hoped that anyone could benefit from the lessons presented herein. I want to emphasize that it is important to read the book in its entirety in order to get the full scope of what I am attempting to present. And, lastly, the reader will soon become aware of a certain amount of repetition. This is by design because this is what occurs in the groups I conduct. The central idea is that when thinking changes, emotions and actions change accordingly. This theme is woven throughout the pages of this book.

IT'S ALL IN THE WAY YOU THINK

PREMISES

PREMISE #1: There is a direct and necessary relationship between language, thinking, emotions and behavior. Understanding this relationship is basic to addressing and alleviating personal problems.

PREMISE #2: Faulty thinking (i.e. illogical, irrational, immature thinking) is the reason for practically all so-called "emotional problems" and socially unacceptable, self-destructive and criminal behavior.

PREMISE #3: While some problems may be psychological or psychiatric (i.e. physical, medical) in nature, many (perhaps most) of the problems people have are more philosophical and/or spiritual in nature. By philosophical I mean logical and ethical; and by spiritual I mean the Greek term psyche (which is most often translated "soul"). Also, I mean spiritual in the broadest sense possible, not a particular religion, denomination or set of doctrines.

PREMISE #4: "Mental illness" is a widely used and generally accepted term that is gradually coming under closer scrutiny. I am using "mental illness" with quotation marks to indicate that I have a problem with the terminology and that I am not using the term in the way it is usually intended. I would replace "mental illness" with "faulty thinking." Again, I am not referring to medical problems which can only be dealt with through medical means. Mind or emotions can hardly become ill, assuming that ill is used in the medical sense to refer to bad health or disease. Thoughts, though, can be faulty in that they can be illogical, irrational, erroneous or immature. "Therapy" (healing), then, is a process of changing faulty thinking to logical, rational, mature thinking.

PREMISE #5: "Mental illness" is basically a choice, a deliberate decision in a particular direction. You literally make up your mind. Regardless of the reasons surrounding the choice, it is nonetheless a choice. Again, this statement would not apply to individuals who are diagnosed with physical/medical problems requiring prescription drugs and/or surgery.

PREMISE #6: Not all "therapy" is therapeutic. The term "therapy" has become increasingly problematic and carries with it some baggage that is neither useful nor even necessary. Actually, therapy means healing and healing almost always has a physical, not a mental, connotation.

PREMISE #7: When thinking changes, emotions and actions (behavior) change accordingly. *The Diagnostic and Statistical Manual* (DSM IV, the psychologists and psychiatrists "Bible") places the emphasis on emotions and behavior (i.e. emotional problems and behavioral problems) in the attempt to define, explain and solve personal problems. However, this approach deals more with symptoms rather than causes as it gets the cart before the horse. It is useless and fruitless to try to change emotions and/or behavior without first changing thinking.

PREMISE #8: In order for thinking to result in appropriate emotions and appropriate actions you must be willing to change the way you think, and also the way you think about thinking (i.e. the thought process). You may think that because you have thought about certain things in certain ways all of your life that there is only one way to think, and that you must continue thinking in this manner. However, you must be willing to think in ways that you have probably never considered before, and which may appear strange and awkward at first.

PREMISE #9: Change in thinking is extremely difficult and, in many cases, not likely to occur to any significant degree; not in the sense that it can't happen, but in the sense that it won't. Change in thinking (at least to the extent that it positively effects emotions and actions) involves realization, decision and resolve. You must recognize the need for change, and then make a decision to change and be able to stay with the program for change. Thinking, emotions and actions are decisions/choices often made capriciously but always deliberately and never without sacrifice. Insight is instant; change can be but may take a while, if ever.

PREMISE #10: Every organism (and organization) usually has within itself the power to heal itself. You may get advice, instruction and inspiration from the outside, but you decide the if-when-how of living your life. In a real sense you do not "get therapy," you create therapy (healing) as you move through the experiences of living day to day in a rational, well-thought way. Furthermore, you alone are responsible for your thoughts, emotions and actions, period. Making excuses, blaming others or "having a bad day" will not work well as explanations for faulty thinking and inappropriate emotions and actions.

SECTION ONE: PROBLEMS

A. Language

"How forceful are honest words." -- Job 6:25

"How good is a word in season." -- Proverbs 15:23

"A word fitly spoken is like apples of gold in a setting of silver." -- Proverbs 25:11

"Let what you say be simply 'yes' and 'no'." – Matthew 5:37

You will be held accountable for uttering careless words; for by your words you will be justified, and by your words you will be condemned." -- Matthew 12:36-37

"Foolish words I can never unsay." -- H.S. Sutton (In other words, you can never take back what you say.)

"It is more important to redeem words than to redeem people." -- Matthew Fox

"Language is not communication of message. It is substance." -- Peter F. Drucker

"Prune your words." -- John Henry Cardinal Newman

"The way we speak is ultimately linked to the way we feel because how we describe the world must at some level reflect how we experience it." -- Alain de Bottom (from *How Proust Can Change Your Life)*

The Danish philosopher and theologian Soren Kierkegaard (1813-1855) preached the sanctity of language. For him language, aesthetics and morality were of equal importance. Goodness and badness, the entire ethical enterprise, begins and ends with language.

For the German philosopher Karl Krause (1874-1936) language is bound up with morality and integrity. To corrupt language is to corrupt individuals and society. Krause equated bad communication with immorality.

How important is language? In a sense it's what makes us human. Imagine trying to exist in a world without language and it becomes immediately clear how important language is. There was a time when one's word was considered sacred. "You have my word on it" was all that was needed to seal contracts, bridge gaps and bind wounds. A "gentleman's agreement" or handshake was the visible symbol of the given word. The need for written contracts, agreements and even warrantees, or for lawyers to process such documents, simply did not exist until relatively recently.

It doesn't take a lot of pondering to realize that as a society we are way past anything that resembles that kind of trust. Not only do we not trust each other at hardly any level, we have great difficulty even understanding each other. This is not because human nature (if there is such a thing) has taken a turn for the worst. It is due to a number of factors which were inevitable given the population growth, increase in technology, industrialization, immigration, globalization, labor specialization and so forth. All of these factors have added to the probability that words would eventually loose some of their meaning and that communication has and will continue to become more difficult. During the past decade alone an entirely new internet vocabulary has developed, and there is little doubt that this phenomenon will repeat itself again and again in the future.

1. Language and the Loss of Liberty

"When language is without an object, no affair can be effected" (from the *Analects of Confucius*, (551-479 B.C.). This statement has been interpreted as: When words loose their meaning, people loose their liberty. Confucius also said: "He who does not understand words is incapable of understanding others." For him the correct use of language is the basis upon which the sociopolitical order is built.

Unfortunately we live in an abbreviated society. We want quick fixes, short cuts and instant everything from food to relationships. We have reduced language down to its lowest common absurdity. The "high-five" has replaced the firmness of the handshake in certain circles thereby devaluing its meaning and importance. We have done much the same thing to language. When a word means something different to everyone it actually means nothing to anyone. I once asked a group of teenagers to define "cool." The variety of definitions was astounding.

The concept of "political correctness" has, in some measure, created more problems than it has solved. Political correctness has conditioned, watered down and otherwise made impotent a lot of ordinary language to the extent that it is difficult to say anything substantial or that makes sense or that has depth of meaning that does not run the risk of inviting criticism and/or at least negative sanctions; or, what is worse, a law suit from some element or segment of society bent on revenge or creating havoc. In certain situations you're damned if you do or don't. For example, from the standpoint of political correctness it is difficult to distinguish legitimate, responsible forms of child discipline (i.e. both positive and negative sanctions) from child abuse. It could be argued that political correctness limit's the accuracy and force of certain words and phrases.

It is indeed possible, as Confucius suggested, that when words loose their meanings, people do, in fact, loose their liberties. For example, if "honesty" is a word that people no longer take seriously, then it tends to loose its meaning and people might be inclined to become less and less honest. Therefore, laws must be invented to make up for the difference between what used to be (honesty) and what has replaced honesty (i.e. dishonesty). And the more laws, the less freedom. Somewhere in this process of words loosing their meanings people may loose a measure of liberty.

Arguably the single most important and influential philosophical movement of the twentieth century is linguistic analysis. Simply, it is the view that philosophical problems arise "from a muddled use of language, and the only way to solve those problems is through a critique or analysis of the language used to express those views" (Ludwig Wittgenstein, 1889-1951). Wittgenstein, who spent his career trying to emphasize the importance of analyzing language, is considered by many to be the most important philosopher of the twentieth century. There were others before and after him who considered language as the true subject of philosophy.

I believe that one of the major problems confronting human beings today is the lack of importance associated with the use of language. One of the most popular majors in colleges and universities is the area of communications. And, yet, this is precisely the area that doesn't seem to make much progress. Not only does there appear to be a global failure to communicate effectively, our own society doesn't seem to communicate well. We use non-sense language, pseudo-logical language and slang that virtually defies understanding. Many articles in scholarly journals are dense and dull when they could easily be otherwise.

Each year words are added to our vocabulary and, thus, to the dictionary which makes them a legitimate, acceptable part of the English language. To a certain extent this is, of course, normal and necessary due to the rapid advances in the sciences and technology, especially in the areas of cyber space/internet and medicine. But my concern goes deeper than language associated with computer, medical and space technology. I am referring to a basic, fundamental loss of language; a loss that diminishes the human spirit and cuts to the heart of much of what it means to be human beings, namely, the ability to communicate clearly, concisely and compassionately; to understand and to be understood; to communicate so that meaning is not minimized and liberty is not lost.

2. Fallacies Relating to the Misuse of Language

It would seem that anything you can do to improve and refine your use of language would, in turn, improve your ability to think more clearly (i.e. more logically, rationally and maturely). And, of course, if your thinking is logical, your emotions and your actions should be more appropriate. An essential part of the equipment of a sound thinker is the ability to use and interpret language accurately. There are at least six fallacies relating to the misuse of language you should be familiar with. (Note: The following fallacies and some of the examples are from Little, Wilson and Moore, *Applied Logic*, Boston: 1955, Houghton Mifflin Company.)

Fallacy #1: Equivocation. This is the use of a word in two different senses; when an inference is drawn from a word whose meaning has been deliberately or inadvertently shifted in the course of an argument. Example: The poet William Wordsworth is said to have remarked, "I believe I could write like Shakespeare if I had a mind to try." His friend Charles Lamb is supposed to have responded, "Yes, nothing is lacking but the mind." The word "mind" is being used here in two different senses. Wordsworth used it to mean inclination, but Lamb shifted the meaning to refer to intelligence.

Fallacy #2: Obfuscation. Obfuscation is using excessive, meaningless or vague words or phrases for the purpose of obscuring or avoiding an issue. What is often called prestige jargon also falls under this category. Product advertisers often use vague terms to try to enhance the image of their product (Example: A certain brand of toothpaste with GL-70). You might think of obfuscation as similar to a dangling participle. Consider this sentence: “Turning down the street the house looked gray in the distance.” Who or what turned down the street? The sentence reads as though the house did. In this case it is relatively easy to understand the meaning, but that’s not always the case. Consider this example taken from a newspaper in an attempt to correct a previous reporting error: “The jury declared that Ms. Jones was not guilty not guilty.” You may think you understand this statement, but can you be sure?

Fallacy #3: Leading question. This refers to a question designed to elicit an answer not intended by the person the question was put to. A question a lawyer might ask a man on the witness stand is a favorite example. The lawyer asks, “Do you still beat your wife?” If the man says “yes,” then he is obviously guilty because he is admitting that he beats his wife. If he answers “no,” he may not immediately think so but he is still admitting guilt. In saying that he does not still beat his wife, the implication is that he used to beat her but, for whatever reason, he no longer beats her. The word “still” creates a leading question which, in this case, may be considered a trap or trick question.

Fallacy #4: Lifting out of context. This fallacy occurs when only a part of a statement is selected in such a way as to give a misleading idea of what was actually said. A favorite misquotation from the Bible is “money is the root of all evil.” What the verse actually says is “the love of money is the root of all evil” (1 Timothy 6:10). There is a tremendous difference between these two statements. A lot of political campaign “mudslinging” involves candidates misquoting each other, or simply and purposely lifting only a part of a sentence or phrase out of context and making it say something that was not intended. This is supposed to make one candidate look good at the expense of another candidate. Unfortunately this dishonest ploy seems to work very well in many instances. It is important to make statements that cannot be easily tampered with, that are grammar “tight.”

Fallacy #5: False obversion is the misuse of contrasts or opposites. An often used example is that of a pharmacy that advertises that its prescriptions are filled by registered pharmacists. While this is true, it should not be taken to mean that prescriptions filled at other pharmacies are not filled by registered pharmacists. In fact, all prescriptions at all pharmacies are required by law to be filled by registered pharmacists. An advertisement that says "we use only fresh ingredients in our pizzas" does not mean that other pizza restaurants do not, but that's the intended message.

Fallacy #6: False conversion means to pivot at the verb and swing the subject into a predicate position (and vice versa). Example: "No monkeys are human beings." The converse would be "no human beings are monkeys." That is a simple, logical conversion. However, some statements turn out to be false when converted. To say that "all freshmen are students" is not true when converted to "all students are freshmen."

3. Pseudo-Rational Terms and Phrases

Everyone makes statements that if taken literally would not be accurate but yet are understood to some degree. The statement, "I saw a car flying down the road," is an example. Statements of this type are generally harmless (even though inaccurate and not logically possible) because they are interpreted within a context that is comprehensible and believable. Such statements are accepted as sensible because the basic meaning is fairly clear. I saw a car which was, in my estimation, moving too fast for safety.

Other language may be more complex. For example, if you tell me that your friend is crazy, and I have never met your friend and have no significant information about her, I may be a little puzzled. I may want to know if your friend is eccentric, delusional, "paranoid schizophrenic," (or any one of over three hundred "mental illnesses" individuals can get labeled with) or simply someone who exhibits an exuberant personality together with a "wild" lifestyle; in other words, someone who might be considered the life of the party who often behaves in unconventional ways. Without knowing your friend I cannot know with any degree of certainty how to evaluate (interpret) your statement that she is crazy.

Language should always be clear and precise if the intended meaning is to be understood. But we can live with metaphors and other literary devices scattered throughout both speech and writing as long as the intended message is accurately received. Poetry is an example of how language can be constructed with great precision, clarity, beauty and even brevity. But language can be worse than useless if it isn't understood as the speaker or writer intended, or if language is taken literally when it shouldn't be. There are some terms and phrases that seem to make sense on the surface because they are used often (even by professionals which tends to give them a degree of legitimacy). In fact, many such terms and phrases are highly problematic. Consider the following examples.

1) "I just didn't think." How many times have you said that or heard someone say it? It sounds legitimate and logical because it is a well-worn excuse. However, it shouldn't take a genius to figure out that you do not do something and then think about it. You think, then you do things. You may reflect on what you did or why you did it after the fact, but you must think before you act. Ruling out what is usually thought of as involuntary or "non-conscious" movements (e.g. batting your eyes, breathing) everything you do is preceded by thought. If you did things without thinking you probably wouldn't live very long. It would be much more accurate to say, "I didn't think logically," or "I didn't consider the various possible outcomes or consequences." But you must think, i.e. you must decide (tell yourself) to do something or you couldn't do it. Thought occurs so rapidly that it is often easy to think that there are instances in which you do not think before acting. But you do, and that's the

point. Thought precedes behavior, not the other way around.

2) "I didn't think; I just reacted." This is simply another version of "I just didn't think." It is quite absurd to even imagine that you could react (or act, which is the same thing. A reaction is still an action) without thinking. Think about what is being said here. It would be like the following scenario: One day you ran into the house, closed the door behind you and went down into the basement. At the time you had no idea why you did this. A few minutes later you heard the roaring sound of an approaching tornado. At that point you thought: that must be why I ran into the house and went down into the basement. I wondered why I did that. Of course, it was because I needed to be in a safe place.

Talk about getting the cart before the horse! The point is, you do not act (or react) without thinking about it and deciding to act in some way. You see and/or hear the tornado moving towards you. And, based upon your knowledge of, and possibly your previous experience with, tornados you realize the potential danger and you decide on an appropriate course of action. This process occurs in the following manner:

Event (E1) - You saw and/or heard the tornado.

Evaluation (E2) - You thought something like this:
Tornados are dangerous; they can damage and destroy property; they can kill people; I should protect myself and others around me.

Emotion (E3) - Fear, worry, maybe panic.

Effect (E4) - You decided to run into the house and go down into the basement.

3) "I just acted on impulse; I really didn't know what I was doing." A dictionary definition of impulse is "an arousing of the mind…to some unpremeditated action." It may be an arousing and it may be unpremeditated (i.e. not much

planning or thought beforehand) but it's still from the mind. "Acting on impulse" is simply another way of saying "I acted." In a sense all actions are "on impulse." Impulse is a "force that starts a body into motion." In other words, the force is the thinking process itself.

4) "I just automatically ___________ (did thus and so)." A man in one of my groups related that he and his girlfriend were dining in a restaurant when a man at a table nearby began winking at his girlfriend. He ignored it the first couple of times, but after the third time he said "I just automatically hit him." I was curious to know about the connection between one man's eye lid and another man's fist. The "connection" is simply that the first man chose/decided to hit the second man. You do not automatically hit someone any more than you automatically mow your lawn or go to the dentist. You decide to do whatever you do. The jealous man's statement may sound good on the surface, but it's merely a poor excuse for bad behavior.

5) "Something just came over me." An incarcerated man stated that the reason why he committed his crime was because "something just came over me." Upon hearing his remark I deliberately began looking up and around the room. I asked him if he had any idea when this something might reappear because I, and possibly the others in the group, didn't want to be anywhere near him when it came over him again. It may come over us too. There's no telling what might happen if this something were to suddenly reappear without warning. What's really amazing is that anyone could give credence to such nonsense. The something that came over him was, of course, a deliberate decision, his choice, to commit a crime.

6) "Something told me to ____________ (do whatever)." How often have you used this little excuse when you couldn't think of anything else to say! You may remember the statement comedian Flip Wilson made famous a few

years ago: "The Devil made me do it." This appears to be the prefect excuse. If that's the case, then he couldn't be held responsible or accountable for his actions. If the Devil (or some other assumed power) made him do it he had no choice; he had to do it. This kind of thinking is not only illogical, it's quite bazaar. Yet, it's often accepted in everyday conversation as a perfectly normal explanation for certain kinds of behavior. The "something" is, of course, yourself thinking, deciding, and acting.

7) "I just made a mistake." This is a commonly used statement which, more often than not, is an excuse for something that didn't turn out well. The truth is, mistakes rarely happen. Car wrecks are not so much accidents as bad decisions. People who commit crimes do not make mistakes, they make bad decisions or choices. A young man in a correctional institution was angry because he was "sent to prison for just one mistake." I asked him, "What was your mistake?" He said, "You know, the reason I am here." "I know why you're here," I replied, "but what is your mistake?" Actually, of course, there was no mistake. The young man did not mistakenly or accidentally rob a store; he chose/decided to rob a store. There's a huge difference. Granted, it was a bad choice, but a choice nonetheless, not a mistake.

8) "It just happened." This excuse is quite interesting, even entertaining. It has an element of mystery about it. One second there's nothing; the next second there's something. Amazing! This is what wives sometimes hear from husbands (or husbands from wives) who get caught in a romantic relationship with another person. "Honey, it really isn't anything. S/he means nothing to me. It just happened." Well, sure. Relationships "just happen" about like war and the bubonic plague just happen. Nothing just happens. And relationships certainly require at least some time to cultivate. On the surface "it just happens" may sound like a legitimate way out of a dilemma. And sometimes it actually works (like

"I was caught off guard"), but you had better not count on it.

9) "It's just the way I am." I had received several complaints regarding the manner in which a correctional officer treated visitors in the visiting room. When I talked with her about her alleged rudeness and lack of tact she replied, "I don't mean anything by what I say; it's just the way I am." Oh, well then; if that's the way she is then, obviously, she shouldn't be held accountable for her behavior. Her situation is similar to "the Devil made me do it." My response to this officer was "I know that's the way you are. That's the problem. I don't want you to be the way you are, I want you to be different" (namely, courteous instead of rude). The officer didn't have to act the way she was. She chose her behavior and she certainly could act differently.

10) "She made me so angry." This is a commonly used statement but it's clearly inaccurate. It may sound sensible because you've heard it and probably used it all your life. The idea is that an event (something, anything) outside of you can make you become angry (or sad, or happy or whatever). However, events (things that happen to you or around you; anything related to your environment) cannot possibly cause or produce emotions. It is impossible for another person, regardless of what she says or does, to make you angry. Look at the ridiculous logic: If someone or something can make you angry, then you actually have no choice in the matter. You must become angry whether you want to or not. You have no control over your emotions. You are simply a victim at the mercy of the person or the thing that is "making" you angry. You are being used like a robot or a puppet by some force beyond your control.

You know almost instinctively that there is a problem with the idea that you have no choice whether or not you become angry. Of course you have a choice. In fact, you use your power of choice to become angry. The other person, regardless of what was said or done, did not and cannot make you angry. How did you become angry? You became angry because of how you evaluated the (any particular) event. Your own thoughts (probably illogical, inaccurate and un-provable) created your anger. (Note: Not all anger is necessarily bad. A discussion on "anger management" will appear in a later section.)

11) "He went off/exploded/clocked." Actually no one ever does any of these things so why use such non-descriptive, inaccurate language in an attempt to describe unacceptable, immature and often violent behavior? On one occasion when an inmate wasn't getting what he wanted he blurted out, "You just want me to go off, don't you!" Much to his surprise I replied, "Yes, as a matter of fact I do." I explained to him that I had often heard of this much talked about phenomenon but I had never actually witnessed someone going off. I asked him to wait until I could get a pen and note pad and a couple of other staff who might also be interested in observing this event. When everyone was ready I said to the inmate who was about to make history, "All right, go ahead." The young man appeared more than a little baffled. I repeated, "We're waiting with anticipation to see how this works out; go ahead and go off." The inmate replied, "You people are crazy," and he walked out of the office (much to my disappointment I might add).

At another time and place a female inmate who spent several days in disciplinary segregation for a rule violation informed me that she was going to explode. When I told her that I had some serious doubts about her ability (and, for that matter, her willingness) to explode, she emphatically insisted that she was going to do it. I said that if she was determined to explode I probably couldn't stop her and that I would simply observe and take some notes. With that, she clinched her fists and screamed for at least a couple of minutes. I stood motionless and waited. When she stopped (as surely she must) I said, "Well, that was a pretty good scream, but I thought you were going to explode." Her response was, "I just did." I reminded her that she looked remarkably intact to me, and that she appeared no worse off for the screaming.

It isn't that I don't take peoples problems seriously. I knew the two inmates just mentioned quite well and I knew how to deal with them. My point is simply that people do not go off, explode or anything similar. So why use that kind of terminology? Why treat someone as if these were actual or potential or even possible conditions? The young man made himself frustrated and angry because he didn't get what he wanted (in this case, to be transferred to a facility he wasn't eligible for; and this had been explained to him). So, as a tactic to try to get what he wanted he became intent on behaving in a threatening, immature and socially unacceptable manner hoping that the staff would decide to transfer him rather than have to deal with his demanding attitude.

The young woman also made herself angry because she had received an incident report and, consequently, was in the segregation unit where she became bored and frustrated. I was not dealing with individuals who were "going off" and "exploding." These are inaccurate, misleading and meaningless terms in relation to the actual situations. I was dealing with angry, frustrated, impatient and socially maladjusted individuals who often talked excessively loud, screamed, threw things and generally behaved in an inappropriate manner in order to get attention and to get what they wanted.

12) "His mind snapped." Some years ago a man with some weapons got into his truck, drove to a McDonald's restaurant and killed some people. On the evening news a psychologist was asked by a reporter from a T.V. station why the man did it. The psychologist replied, "His mind just snapped." Well, that may sound like a legitimate and accurate statement until you realize how utterly stupid it is. Craniums may crack and blood vessels may break but minds do not snap. Think about

it. Have you ever known anyone with a mind-snapping problem? Does your mind snap occasionally? If so you had better see a M.D. or perhaps a chiropractor, but not a Ph.D.

The man at McDonald's, for whatever reason, chose to shoot people. Certainly he was not thinking logically/rationally that day. But his terrible action was not because his mind snapped. If that were the case, at what point did it actually happen? If it occurred while he was driving to McDonald's why didn't he have a wreck, or maybe decide to go to the hospital? He could have done any number of things beside what he did. The man chose his actions. He did not "snap," or "go off," or "get pushed over the edge" (another little gem often used as an excuse for someone's negative or abhorrent behavior).

13) "I have a short fuse." This probably falls into a similar category with people who go off, explode, have minds that snap, and the like. Labeling someone who immediately or quickly makes himself angry without considering other more logical options as having a "short fuse" is as ridiculous as the improper behavior itself. This is yet another excuse for inappropriate, obnoxious behavior. Is everyone supposed to put up with an angry, abusive, disruptive and possibly dangerous person because he has a "short fuse?" It's nothing short of amazing how such really stupid language is often accepted as legitimate.

14) "I bottle up my feelings." Whenever I hear this statement I usually ask the person to show me exactly how she does it. The fact is that people have grown so accustomed to saying and listening to such non-sense statements that they aren't immediately aware of how silly and illogical (not to mention impossible) they really are. It may take a while to become aware of what is actually being said. Obviously no one bottles up feelings. So, then, what does one actually do? Maybe what is really being said is that "I don't talk about or otherwise try to deal with certain

unpleasant situations that happen in my life." But, in any case, "bottling up feelings" does not accurately describe whatever is happening.

15) "I couldn't help myself." A teen-age girl used this excuse for shoplifting in a drug store. When she saw all those cosmetics she filled her pockets, and she got caught. But don't you feel sorry for her? After all she couldn't help herself. A woman who persistently wrote bad checks and ended up in prison told me that she couldn't help it; she could not stop herself from writing checks knowing that there was no money in the bank. Consider what is being said here. The girl could not not take the items. The woman could not not write bad checks. In neither case was the judge impressed by these lame excuses for criminal behavior. Being out of control (if that is what it is) is still a choice.

16) "Her remark triggered his reaction." The word "triggered" is used a lot nowadays in a variety of contexts. In reference to or as a description of human behavior it is bad terminology. As a natural phenomenon lightening (which is caused by other processes) may trigger thunder (assuming that trigger means cause). That is, because of the lightening the thunder must occur. Or, if the trigger of a gun is pulled the round must fire (assuming that all the mechanics are operating properly). However, your behavior is not triggered in the sense that it must occur as a consequence or a result of the prior behavior of someone or something else. That is, behavior on the part of one person does not "trigger" (cause) the behavior of another person. If someone makes a negative or insulting remark, you are not obliged to respond in a negative manner. Actually, you are not obliged to respond in any way at all. A remark cannot "trigger" some kind of response whether you want to respond or not. Thunder and bullets have no choice, but you most certainly do.

The faulty logic here should be obvious. When something happens (i.e. actions, statements) there are any number of responses (or possibly no responses at all) which can occur. When lightening occurs it is always and almost immediately followed by thunder. It has no choice. But human behavior is chosen. The word "triggered" is misleading and perverts an accurate evaluation of events. "Triggered" may be an appropriate and accurate (if not technical or scientific) term when applied to certain phenomenon or mechanical devices. But it is a pseudo-logical term if it is used to attempt to describe human behavior. Example: A man in a substance abuse program stated that the death of his aunt triggered his starting to use drugs again. Now, get the picture. His aunt lived 2000 miles away. He hadn't seen her for years and had never had a close relationship with her. Yet, the news of her death "triggered" his return to using drugs. Apparently this man was looking for an excuse and the news of the death of his aunt provided it.

17) "James is struggling with drugs." I read in the newspaper one day that a professional athlete was "struggling with drugs." Struggle/struggled/struggling are also terms that are overused and misused a lot. Basketball and football teams who aren't winning are often said to be struggling. Individuals who aren't functioning up to their own or someone else's expectations may be said to be struggling. Actually, this may or may not be the case. Struggle should indicate an intense effort against great obstacles. It isn't the same as goofing off, inattention, irresponsibility, carelessness, lack of preparation, lack of self-control, a bad attitude, poor timing, errors in judgment and so on. Struggling should not be a synonym for failure to achieve. If an athlete (or anyone else) is "having a bad season," is he struggling or simply not working hard enough? Of course there can be circumstances beyond ones control, but bad decisions and poor performance is not the same as struggling.

A big part of the problem with using the word struggle to describe failure is that it can elicit sympathy where none is due. You may tend to feel sorry for someone who is said to be "struggling" as though that individual is doing the best he can do under trying and adverse circumstances, when, in fact, that may not be the case at all. Failure does not usually result from struggle. In fact, quite the opposite. Those who struggle are probably more likely to finally succeed.

So, what about James who is "struggling with drugs?" Is he using or not? At first it may appear that James is doing everything he can to stop using drugs. Isn't that what struggle implies? But when you examine the statement more closely it becomes apparent that little actual, factual information is given about what is going on with James. All that can be known for certain is that he is "struggling with drugs." If he is still using, maybe he isn't struggling hard enough. One either uses drugs or one doesn't, but one hardly struggles with drugs.

18) "It's been an emotional day." More will be said about emotion in another section. Suffice it to say at this point that "emotion/emotional" are overused, misused and abused words. The word "emotion(al)" tells virtually nothing about the condition or the behavior of the particular person or persons in question. Does emotional describe happiness, sadness, anger, laughter, violence, or what? Saying that someone was emotional is like saying there was weather. And referring to an occasion as emotional is like talking about a happy rock or a worried tree. People may exhibit emotions (either positive or negative) but the fourth of July can never be an emotional day. By the way, emotion and behavior are the topics many therapists focus on. The problem, of course, is that thinking, which produces both and which should be the primary focus, may never be mentioned.

There are many more terms and phrases that could be listed. (For example: "She knows how to push my button.") All of the above are illogical, incorrect. Yet, because they are so widely used and often repeated they sound valid and sensible. When the language you use is illogical, the emotion(s) that follow will invariably be inappropriate. And, consequently, your actions will usually be inappropriate. It is important to remember that events, regardless of what they are, do not cause emotions. Evaluation of events causes emotions. If an event were totally ignored (i.e. you didn't think about it at all) you would have no emotion at all. The objective is not to try to have no emotions; rather to have appropriate emotions followed by appropriate actions based upon logical, mature thinking. To state the "formula" again:

Events (E1) are things that happen. (Anything, everything, whatever).

Evaluation (E2) is your interpretation of events, either logically or illogically.

Emotion (E3) is created by you only at this point.

Effect (E4) is what finally happens as a result of all the above.

4. Frustration Statements

A dictionary definition of frustration is "to induce feelings of insecurity, discouragement, or dissatisfaction." Probably a better definition is "to bring to nothing." Frustration statements are not inherently wrong or necessary harmful. If you miss the nail and hit your finger with the hammer you are likely to express your frustration or pain with a four letter word ("ouch," "damn"). If the doctor tells you to let her know if it hurts, you will almost certainly oblige with an appropriate word. Such expressions may actually be helpful because you are experiencing and reflecting a physical condition which may be useful or necessary to your health, safety and security. This is one example of expressing frustration and its understanding is rather elementary.

There are other frustration statements that are more problematic and deserve a closer look. These are statements that have nothing to do with physical discomfort, but which are useless and actually harmful not only to your self-image but in building rapport and positive relationships with others. Such statements tend to reflect the second definition, “to bring to nothing.” Some examples are:

I hate you.

Go to hell.

Shut up and leave me alone (the kid at camp with Charlie Brown).

You’re nothing but a yellow, god damned, SOB.

I hope you perish, bitch.

The list could go on and on, but you get the picture. Incidentally, I have heard all of these frustration statements many (too many) times.

In looking at these examples, the rational thinking person will find them ridiculous or maybe even humorous. In a sense these kinds of remarks are harmless. They are a poor choice of words, not “sticks and stones.” You would rather not have to listen to such statements or to put up with those who make them. But you have heard them dozens of times and have probably used them yourself on certain occasions.

Upon rational reflection, are you harmed in any way? Are you any worse off? Are you really any different because someone says they hate you? Are you really going to seriously consider the injunction to go to hell just because someone with a bad disposition, not to mention bad manners, suggest it? Since it isn’t biologically possible for a human being to be the offspring of a dog, the expression S.O.B. is false and frivolous. You know that, so why in the world would you upset yourself if someone referred to you in such a starkly inaccurate and crude manner?

There are at least three things you need to remember about frustration statements. First, they are totally ineffective in dealing with the situation at hand. The choice of words is unrelated to the problem. Frustration statements are a total waste of time and energy. Second, the person making the statement is making more of a statement about himself than about the person the statement is directed towards. In other words, he is demonstrating, in dramatic fashion, that he is at his wits end, that he can think of nothing rational or appropriate to say, and that he is out of control. Taking all these factors together, frustration statements appear completely out of place, and the person making the statements loses credibility. Like the coyote trying to catch the roadrunner, the intended damage gets turned back upon the originator of the frustration statement. Third, frustration statements invite further escalation of an already bad (or apparently so) situation. If a frustration statement is directed towards a person who recognizes the nature of the situation and who remains calm and rational, the damage or effect may be minimal or zero. However, if such a statement is directed towards someone who is in the same frame of mind as the person making the statement, the situation is likely to become worse. The "I will get even" notion may come into play.

The important question to ask is who has the problem? If the person the frustration statement was directed towards evaluates the event (i.e. thinks about what was said) in a logical, mature manner the problem may end right there. When you realize that a person is saying things that are indicative of one who is frustrated and out of control, the best course of action is to calmly back off and allow that person time to regain his composure. If the offending person is actually a friend or associate, simply leave him alone. In all likelihood he will eventually come to his senses and straighten himself out. If the offending person is a stranger, someone hardly known or not known at all; or someone who is known for irrational behavior, leave him alone also. In either case, there's probably nothing you can do or say that will help or change anything anyway.

B. Therapy

1. A Sea of Therapy

Our American society is drowning in a sea of therapy. We are bombarded and saturated with the idea that every problem, no matter how large or small, needs some kind of "therapeutic intervention." We are so addicted to the notion of therapy that we think we need help from a "professional" because we cannot solve our own problems, nor are we expected to. After all, we aren't qualified to find solutions to our own problems. In times of public or national crisis one of the first orders of business is to send in the therapist. We have become a nation of victims who either need a lawyer to process litigation for "mental suffering" (for which exorbitant sums of money seem to bring instant, miraculous cures) and/or therapist who help us to "find ourselves," "get in touch with our feelings," and who often ask virtually meaningless questions such as "how do you feel about that," or "how does that make you feel?"

We have become a therapeutic community. We have been "trained" and sensitized to depend upon someone or something to rescue us, or at least explain away everything from unpleasant and distasteful things we simply do not want to be bothered with to catastrophic events. We have little or no self-reliance (a major theme of Ralph Waldo Emerson), or analytical and critical skills. When unpleasant events occur, counselors ("grief counselors") arrive on the scene to administer "therapy," which can be a good thing but which often attempts to either explain away or exaggerate and exacerbate the perception of the situation.

The general premise among many counselors seems to be that if individuals talk ("express their feelings") to someone who is "trained to listen," then therapy has occurred. And there is little doubt that talking and listening is, or can be, part of the therapeutic process. In many cases it is the place to start; and it is helpful, at least for the short term. Getting some attention is not necessarily a bad thing. But has anything really changed? Has any long term or permanent benefits been achieved? Well, of course, it is hard to say. You can feel better, at least for a while, without actually getting better.

So, counselors/therapists encourage talking. And then what? There was a book published a few years ago entitled, *What Do You Say After You Say Hello*? Well, in this case, what do you say or do after you state how you feel? What do you do after you express your emotions, vent your feelings, get in touch with your feelings and discover your inner self? Is that the gist of therapy? It is unfortunate that many therapists never seem to get beyond the feeling stage. They ask you how you feel but they may never get around to finding out the basis for your feelings. The fact is, of course, that you feel however you think. Focusing on feelings is merely dealing with the symptom rather than the cause. Legitimate therapy must begin with examining faulty thinking.

Therapy basically means healing. The koine Greek verb therapeuo and the noun therapia both mean healing, caring, attending to. And healing is directly related to knowledge, which has to do with thinking. The primary goal of therapy ought to be to get in touch with your thinking. And "touch" probably is not the best term. "Examine," in the Socratic sense, is perhaps a better term. In any case, if your thinking is clear, logical and mature, your feelings and, consequently, your behavior, will be positively impacted. The first step in therapy involves trying to understand your pattern of thinking and its consequences. If your thinking has led you to inappropriate emotions and actions, then it would seem to follow that the emphasis should be on changing the way you think.

It is possible to be in therapy up to your ears for years without experiencing any real, authentic change in emotions or behavior. This is one of the reasons why therapy as usual is gradually coming under a lot of scrutiny. Many are beginning to question the value of therapy which not only can be very expensive but often belies logic. For example, with behavior modification the assumption is that behavior can change without changing the thinking that produces behavior in the first place. This is almost as ridiculous as expecting a light to come on, then flipping the switch. On the surface, and for very short periods of time, behavior modification may be instrumental in accomplishing certain specific, simple, immediate goals. However, as a strategy for achieving long-range, permanent change in behavior it is woefully inadequate. And the reason is quite simply: change in behavior does not occur until change in thinking occurs; that is, until faulty, illogical thinking is replaced with mature, logical thinking.

A therapist cannot successfully work from the premise that the goal is to change behavior or help an individual feel better. The reason why individuals go to therapists over long periods of time and never seem to get "cured" is that the therapist may be working from the faulty premise or assumption that the goal is to help people feel better, and that feeling better is the same as getting better. The emphasis, instead, should be on cognitive change, not on feelings or behavior. When thinking is on the right track emotions and behavior will follow. "Feeling better" kind of therapy is, at best, a band aid. Real therapy may involve radical mind surgery.

If you want to feel better and behave more responsibly, then you need to discover a way to change the way you think. You need a method that works; you need a "track" to run on. To begin with you need to be willing to not only change the way you think, but to change the way you think about thinking (i.e. about the thinking process itself, which may be quite different from the way you usually think). The overall message of this book (which is stated several times and in various ways) is that when your thinking changes (becomes more logical and mature), your emotions (almost invariably) become more appropriate; and, consequently, your actions (behavior, whatever you decide to do) will become more appropriate. Event Evaluation Training offers you a highly effective way of working this out.

2. Language and Therapy

Much of the problem with the language used by many therapists has its origin in society itself. We seem comfortable with fuzzy, vague, imprecise language. We don't seem to like being pinned down by facts and statistics. In times past language was more clearly defined and delineated. Nowadays we seem to prefer imprecision, vagueness, fogginess and "maybe." Politicians on the campaign trail may not like to give actual answers (almost never yes or no) to questions. They know that regardless of what they say some will agree and others will not. So they may attempt to take a safe, middle path which often results in saying virtually nothing. Even corporate logos and familiar icons which used to be clearly representative and easily identified and understood now look more like impressionistic art or something put together by a committee of kindergartners. We expect everyone to be politically correct but we don't want to get to the point. Why? Well, perhaps there is no point to get to. But more likely it is because of the fear of taking a stand and being labeled. And labels are sometimes hard to peel off. Taking a stand is risky business because possibilities become minimized while responsibility becomes maximized.

Trying to make sense of terms such as multiculturalism, globalization and deconstruction is not an easy task for many. Political correctness, for example, as a concept has several inherent problems. As it relates to therapy political correctness strongly implies that virtually everyone is some sort of victim. Victims, obviously, need help (therapy). And therapy is often an attempt to "treat" symptoms (emotions and behavior) rather than the cause (faulty thinking). According to the DSM (Diagnostic and Statistical Manual) there is probably not a person on the face of the earth who does not have some sort of "mental illness." The list of "mental disorders" and "behavioral problems" is amazing. Recently I read about an "illness" I was unaware of: "Generalized Anxiety Disorder." I was reminded of the passage in Acts 17:23 (New Testament). The Apostle Paul visited Athens and saw an idol "to an unknown god." So, if you can't nail it down, don't ignore it. This category should catch it.

Diagnosis basically means to discover the problem. But the problem is always the same: faulty thinking, wrong inferences, incorrect conclusions based on false premises. So much psychotherapy deals with symptoms rather than causes. That is, starting with emotions/feelings is not the right approach since the root cause of the problem is faulty, illogical thinking. And, in the same way, starting with attempting to change behavior (e.g. behavior modification) without first addressing the faulty thinking that eventually results in unacceptable, destructive behavior is simply not possible. Therefore, a proper diagnosis would be an examination of the thinking/reasoning process. But, alas! The Diagnostic and Statistical Manual diagnoses emotional and behavioral problems as though they were somehow divorced from thinking. Emotions are generated by thinking. Behavior is a consequence of thinking, with emotion as a contributing factor to one degree or another. So, the only thing left to diagnose is thinking. And logic offers the proper tools for diagnosis (i.e. evaluation of events).

Think of the "craziest" person you've ever met. Assuming that that individual has no physical or medical conditions that would contribute to an irrational state of mind, what is the problem with this person? You can diagnose, gather statistics, talk, listen, reflect and "treat" all you want, but you're still looking at a person whose thinking is illogical. That's the problem. And unless you can help this person to change his thinking to a more logical/rational/mature level no change in emotion or behavior is likely to occur.

I remember a man I met in a correctional institution who sent messages by birds to individuals who lived over 200 miles away. He also believed he had the ability to keep airplanes from running into each other by making certain gestures with his hands and by giving mental commands to the pilots. Now, what is the proper diagnosis for this individual (who, by all stretches of the imagination isn't behaving normally), and how can he be "treated?" Given that he has no physical or medical condition which required medical attention, the problem is that his thinking is wrong. The task of the therapist/counselor/case manager is to try to help him change his way of thinking; to help him understand that sending messages by birds to his family 200 miles away is not the best way to communicate with them, and that there is a highly unlikely connection between his actions on the ground and the movement of airplanes in the air. In other words, his faulty thinking must be challenged. If that doesn't work over a reasonable period of time, then probably nothing is going to work until he himself decides to get back to reality.

3. Wrong Questions, Wrong Objective

The following is a list of some of the objectives of some therapists.

1) "Helping people feel good about themselves." While on a trip in my car I listened to a radio program which included an interview with a child psychologist. When asked by the interviewer what is the primary job of a child psychologist he replied: "The primary job of a child psychologist is to make children feel good about themselves." Now, if this is really the job of child

psychologists they are bound to fail for at least two reasons. First, a psychologist (nor anyone else for that matter) cannot "make" anyone feel good about herself. The very notion sounds somewhat tyrannical. It's like saying that you're going to have to feel good about yourself whether you want to or not. Second, feeling good about oneself is a by-product, a result of other factors (e.g. accomplishment, a certain measure of success in some endeavor, good grades, good relationships with significant others, religious faith), and not necessarily from talking about feeling good about oneself. Trying to make a child (or an adult) feel good about herself is, again, attempting to address the symptom rather than the cause(s).

Incidentally (or perhaps not so incidentally) children would likely "get over it" sooner except for therapists who, in some instances, won't let them turn it loose. Therapists/counselors often "catastrophize" events, thus causing the evaluation process to become more difficult and skewed. They keep the problem alive unnecessarily rather than help children face the reality of the situation, and help them understand that we live in a world where good and evil exist side by side, where bad things sometimes happen to good people and good things sometimes happen to bad people. And it isn't a matter of who deserves or didn't deserve what, nor is it a matter of fairness. It's simply the way the world is. Children are not helped by sugar-coating tragedy in the name of "therapy," nor by being asked leading questions. If grief is natural and normal (and indeed it is), then it should be connected to the tragic event.

2) "You need to work through your feelings." So many times I am told by clients that they have been instructed by their therapist to work through their feelings. Many try to do just that but end up quite frustrated. You cannot "work through" your feelings without examining (working through?) your thinking, which, of course, is

where you must begin in the first place. The kind of therapy process many therapists advocate can take years on the false premise that since it took a long time to get to a state of "mental illness," or that you have been "mentally ill' for a long time or you have had your problem for a long time, it will, therefore, take a long time to "heal." This is simply not true. Insight is instant. And "healing" can occur extremely rapidly once thinking changes. Actually, you change (heal) when you decide to change, however long that may take. "Working through" or "processing feelings" may take a lot of time and a lot of money. And, if that's all you're doing, you're probably going in circles because little will be gained without first examining the thinking process that produces emotions and actions.

3) "How did/does that make you feel?" The question is how does a statement or action on the part of someone else make you feel? It is, of course, the wrong question? And if it's the wrong question, coming up with the right answer is not likely. "That" or "it" didn't make you feel anything. Events do not create emotions. And even if events did create emotions, what difference would it make how the event made you feel? A better question might be: What, exactly, is the problem; and what are your options for dealing with it in a way you can live with? You might, first of all, ask yourself: Is it really a problem? Whose problem is it? Is it worth time and effort? But, in any case, you feel basically however you choose to feel based upon your evaluation of the event(s). You are in control. You are not bound by someone or some-thing "making" you feel good or bad.

4) "I just want to help people get in touch with their feelings." Well, here we go again. A psychologist, who wanted to volunteer to conduct a therapy group for men, told me that his job as a group therapist was to "help people get in touch with their feelings." Granted, this

may sound like a noble undertaking until you realize that it's what's commonly referred to as an exercise in futility. The problem is very similar to number 3 above. Helping people get in touch with their feelings is the wrong point of departure. In the first place, why would you want to get in touch with your feelings? What if you feel bad, sad, angry, hopeless, disgusted, mean or hateful? Now what? It's fine to identify your emotion(s) if your objective is to discover where it/they originated, and understand that emotions don't land on you from somewhere outside yourself and cause you to do strange or bad things. Even if you "get in touch" with your feelings you'll probably continue to feel the same way until you change your thinking from negative, illogical thoughts to more positive, mature, logical thoughts. Your feeling at any given moment is due to your evaluation of the events in your life. If "getting in touch" means getting your thinking straight, then fine. Otherwise, what's there to get in touch with? And, why? Don't waste your time trying to fix your emotions.

5) "Recovery - Closure - Healing." Terms such as therapy, emotion(al), recovery, closure, heal(ing), struggle(ing) are used ad nauseaum nowadays. Following some tragic event you may hear "let the healing process begin." I'm sorry to say this often means let the dollars flow. It's amazing how often "closure" or "healing" is preceded by monetary settlements. Does a "get even" mentality followed by litigation produce closure and healing? One would certainly think so in many cases.

Closure occurs whenever you decide to close it. When the perpetrator of a violent act is found guilty (and especially in certain instances where the death sentence is given) the victim's family or close friends may be said to have closure at last. In other words, closure very often is equated with vengeance, which, by the way, happens to be a thoroughly un-Christian notion. (I mention this simply because I see no basic difference in the way in which those who consider themselves Christians and those who aren't Christians view legal and moral issues.) My point is simply that, in spite of tragic events that may have deep and abiding impact on the lives of certain individuals, closure and/or healing occurs as the result of a rational, mature thought process of deciding to "let it go" and move on with life.

6) "She needs treatment." Treatment is basically a medical term (as is heal or healing). A physician renders treatment. In what sense do therapists render treatment? Treatment, as rendered by therapists, for the most part, involves talking and listening. And unless most of the talk is about how to change faulty thinking to logical thinking not a lot will be gained.

To summarize, a lot of therapy is ineffectual for the following reasons (most of which have to do with language):

Often the wrong questions are asked. Asking how you feel or why you did such and such will get no useful response. Asking questions that accurately identify the problem and what you are going to do about it require responses that are both positive and pro-active.

Some therapists focus on emotions, i.e. trying to change the way you feel, trying to get you to feel better about yourself. That is virtually impossible considering that feelings come from thoughts.

Some therapists focus on behavior, i.e. trying to change behavior (e.g. behavior modification).That is also virtually impossible considering that behavior is a consequence of thoughts.

Some therapists simply attempt to pacify the client, i.e. try to help the client fulfill some outrageously unattainable objective by offering "support" rather than confronting the client's illogical, fanciful or self-destructive thinking pattern. A counselor once told me that his job was to keep his clients happy. That is, the objective was simply to help the client get to where she wants to be. I'm sure that viewpoint does not describe all therapists/counselors, but it probably does describe many. Think about it: if physicians operated by this "principle" they would write prescriptions for whatever kind of drugs the patient wanted regardless of diagnosis. And, unfortunately, according to reports from newspapers and other sources, this also happens. But, of course, it shouldn't. Truth and honesty between counselor and client ought to be a given.

Some therapists see their role as leading the client toward "self-realization," helping clients to reach their "full potential." I'm not sure what this means exactly but it sounds good. I suppose the overriding question is how would you know if you realized yourself and/or if you reached your full potential? Or, even how close you were to that point?

All of the above try to deal with symptoms rather than the causes. And the cause is always the same: faulty thinking. The objective should be to discover a path that leads to more logical, clear, mature thinking. Event Evaluation Training (Therapy) accomplishes that objective.

4. Does Traditional Therapy Help or Hinder?

It may seem strange to suggest that a lot of what happens in the name of therapy today may actually hinder the "healing process." Yet, a closer examination reveals that this may indeed be the case. On a more microscopic level the following is what I believe are some of the problems with therapy in the traditional or usual sense.

First, the most glaring problem is the focus on feelings and behavior rather than on thinking. In fact, this is the core of the problem and I try to discuss it in various ways. Related to this is the problem of asking the wrong questions (e.g. how do you feel about this or that rather than examining the thinking process, patterns of thinking that produce negative emotions and unacceptable, destructive, possibly violent behavior). The right questions should be what are you thinking and how can you bring your thoughts to a higher, more logical and mature level? Traditional therapy often sentimentalizes rather than actualizes events/situations. Asking how something "made you feel" tends to shift responsibility to that which "made" you feel a particular way. Recognizing who is responsible for what and why is an important part of the therapeutic process.

Traditional therapy often prolongs/stretches out the process with unnecessary steps or methods. Consider this statement from a distraught mother regarding her daughter: "It will take months, maybe even years of therapy to get her through this." Her daughter was abducted and released, with no physical harm, after two days. Now, why would the mother make such a statement? In large part, I think, due to being educated for many years by the therapeutic community. She immediately assumed, without much evidence other than what she had been told repeatedly and led to believe, that her daughter was probably traumatized to the point of needing endless months or years of "treatment" from a therapist. Therapy may take the form of assuring the daughter that everyone understands how terrible this ordeal must have been for her, that it wasn't her fault (good up to this point), and then going through an endless litany of questions about how she feels about this and that; and then, possibly week after week, talking about the same things over and over. Obviously different individuals will handle situations differently depending upon the severity of the situation, how accurately and maturely one evaluates (interprets) the event, and so on. And, certainly, nothing that is or is even potentially harmful should ever be minimized.

But there are clearly at least two ways to proceed in dealing with the abducted daughter. On the one hand, the terribleness of the event can be emphasized which, of course, will affect (and even suggest) her own sense of what happened. If everyone around her sees this event as a giant catastrophe, something that she will have to really work at for a long time in order to get over, she will likely be bothered with it for a long time. On the other hand (and which to me seems the more reasonable course) it could be suggested by her mother, her therapist and others close to her that: a) what happened was a bad thing; it could have been worse, and everyone is glad she is safe now and hopes it will never happen again; b) but things like this sometimes happen and you must be ready to understand the situation and decide what needs to be done in order to effect a positive solution, to do what is necessary to prevent future occurrences; and c) most importantly, to suggest that you can't let bad things that happen to you become the defining factors in your life. As terrible as some things are, they have to be put in their place. Actually, you can learn from such events and even become a stronger and better person if you take the "high road" (i.e. the logical rather than sentimental road) to dealing with adversity.

It is wrong, possibly even damaging, to suggest to someone (especially a child) that, as a matter of course, it takes a long time to get over a bad event. A child or young person should never be stuck with the notion that they will have to carry around the baggage of a bad event for the rest of his life. An objective in therapy should be to help individuals think more rationally, realistically and maturely about events (whatever they are), and let emotions and actions take a natural, and probably more appropriate course.

Insight is instant. Change can be instant or it may take longer depending upon a number of possible factors: the evaluation of the event, the evaluation of the way you think others perceive the event, whether you see yourself as a victim, your perception/understanding of the role of therapy and to what extent you believe you need therapy, and the like. But, in any case, the idea that you must continually, and over long periods of time, talk about your feelings about a particular event, is not only misleading, it is usually unproductive and might even be counterproductive. (This is one reason why some people depress themselves for long periods of time.) Such an approach can keep alive, prolong and even intensify the problem. Events should be real-ized but not awful-ized.

The idea that you must have a therapist (professional help) in order to get to the root of your problem (which, of course, is faulty thinking) is simply not true. Such thinking, first of all, diminishes the fact that you have an innate ability to understand and find solutions to your own problems. Sometimes assistance may be needed, or at least helpful, but it is usually assistance in sorting out the thinking process, not in trying to deal with emotions. Except for the most unusual of cases and circumstances, people have the ability to heal themselves. Even the idea that you must have someone to talk to in order for therapy to occur is inaccurate. It is all right, and probably good in most cases, but certainly not necessary. Evaluation of events (interpretation, "self-talk") if properly understood and employed, is the engine for therapy. You feel basically however you decide to feel, and you do whatever you decide to do.

Traditional therapy often exaggerates and exacerbates instead of identifying and clarifying. The truth is that many therapists (or at least the therapeutic process employed) sometimes make situations (events) appear worse than they actually are. An incident that was unfortunate and potentially dangerous may be made to appear catastrophic, awful, terrible, and psychologically fatal. And, what may be worse, is the idea that "you'll never get over this," or "it's going to take a long, long time to get over this." The therapist may not use those words but the idea may get conveyed. The end result will probably be basically the same regardless of whether you "have therapy" or not. Like the common cold, you can take aspirin or not take aspirin; you will likely get over your cold in a reasonable period of time.

It is the quality of therapy, not the quantity or the time element that is the important consideration. Traditional therapy often keeps the "wound" open rather than letting it heal by itself. Resilience is a powerful but sometimes disregarded factor. The problem in a nutshell is that we, as a society, have become indoctrinated toward thinking that we need some kind of therapy for every little whim and whine. Listen: there are millions (probably billions) of people all over the world, who have problems that most of us would have trouble even trying to imagine, who never see a therapist. And, for the majority of these people, what would a therapist do anyway?

5. What About Treatment?

Individuals with "mental health" problems go to therapists for "treatment." So, what exactly is treatment? Obviously, it depends upon several factors such as the type of training the therapist has received and the particular framework (model, approach) from which the therapist works. However, from the standpoint of philosophical counseling "treatment" is largely about helping people change faulty thinking to more logical, rational thinking. This process would also normally involve "naming" the problem (i.e. identifying and stating in the form or a sentence or two what the problem is), and working out possible solutions (and eventually a solution) to the problem. There are a variety of strategies which may be utilized. But if therapy is to occur, treatment must involve a change in thinking with the resulting benefit of more appropriate emotions and more appropriate actions than was the case prior to therapy.

Therapists/counselors are taught to be good listeners, to skillfully hear what the client is saying, and not saying. And the other side of the coin is that clients are encouraged to talk, to "get it off their chest." Especially for individuals who have committed acts of violence toward others, confession is probably the best place to start. Talking and listening are certainly important components of treatment and, consequently, of therapy. But it is only part of the picture. Unfortunately, this is as far as many therapists go. Treatment in this manner becomes circular and can go on for weeks, months, and even years, often with little progress. In fact, if this approach were successful there would be no need for endless months or years of therapy. If treatment is one person sitting for an hour a week telling another person what she has done during the past week, then I doubt that much has been accomplished. The question is: Has the client's thought process changed from faulty, irrational, immature thinking (which created the problem in the first place) to a more logical, mature thinking? Simply talking (or "venting" which is blowing air) may be therapeutic as far as it goes, but unless it is geared toward clearing up foggy thinking it isn't likely to be of much help in the long run.

C Mental Illness

1. The Problem with Mental Illness

Every now and then someone tries to point out the problem with "mental illness," but usually to no avail because our society has become so saturated with psychological jargon that little attention is paid. Again, "mental illness" is the wrong term to describe what might best be called faulty thinking. A brain can become sick (damaged, diseased) but a mind cannot become ill (or sick). The mind is not attached to the brain. A thought cannot become diseased. It can be wrong, stupid, ignorant, or whatever, but not sick. Faulty thinking, no matter how bad, is not mental illness. Faulty thinking (i.e. reaching invalid conclusions) and inappropriate emotions accompanied by inappropriate actions/behavior is hardly a medical condition. It would certainly be a step in the right direction to stop using medical terminology to try to describe or diagnose faulty thinking. Logic cannot be "medicalized." And, after all, what is the problem with an individual often described as paranoid, schizophrenic, delusional, neurotic, or psychotic? The problem (unless it is physical in nature and requires medical attention) relates to and stems from faulty, illogical thinking.

The term "mental illness" sounds legitimate because it has a history and it is a part of everyday usage. Its legitimacy, or even its usefulness, is rarely questioned, and only then usually by some philosophers and sociologists. But it is a term that needs to be examined and redefined (if a redefinition is actually possible). The simplest question to begin with is how can the mind (i.e. thinking, thoughts) be or become ill/sick/diseased? Granted the word "ill" can be defined fairly broadly. But, in any case, ill should not refer to the mind or the thinking process. Thinking, along with writing and conversation, can be described in various ways: prose, poetry, symbolism, parable, metaphor, satire, euphemism, and so on, depending upon the intention of the individual doing the thinking, writing or conversing. But regardless of what is going on, it can hardly be or become ill. If the term "mental illness" could be dispensed with, what term could be used? I believe a far more appropriate term would be, simply, faulty (wrong, muddy, illogical, irrational, immature) thinking.

Mental means that which is or relates to the mind. As I have already pointed out, mind and brain are two different terms. Obviously the mind and the brain relate (that relationship has been and still is one of the most difficult of all philosophical problems). Thinking could not occur without the brain. Yet, the mind and the brain are just as mysteriously unrelated as they are related. While it is possible for the brain to be diseased or to function improperly due to some physiological problem, it is quite impossible for the mind to be or become ill. Thus, "mental illness" is actually a nonsense term.

What is often, and incorrectly, referred to as "mental illness" is actually extended/prolonged/sustained denial of reality. Being mistaken or wrong for a very short period of time is normal. It's easy to think illogically/irrationally. But a mature person will soon recognize faulty thinking and correct it. Otherwise one might continue in a state of reality denial for a long period of time. "Mental illness" is a choice of a state one can or would rather live in than the real or actual one. It is a state (a "world") that can be more easily understood, simplified, rectified, justified and managed than the world one actually lives in. For some individuals the world, for whatever reason, becomes unbearable, so they create their own world. Some may return to the real world (at least for certain periods of time). Some never do. Others may go back and forth.

Whatever one may choose to call it, "mental illness" is a choice. As Sam Keen writes in his book *Beginnings Without End*, "madness is a choice, a decision about a direction, a way of not being in the world." Unless an individual has a physical problem or condition which can only be treated medically, "mental illness" must be a choice. It isn't something external that descends upon or envelopes the mind like some diabolical power. It isn't forced either by events or circumstances. Rather, it is an evaluating, a processing which occurs by irrational thinking. In short, whatever condition that can be ascribed or assigned to the mind is by choice. It may be a choice between undesirables, but a choice nonetheless. If your thinking is faulty and, consequently, your emotions and actions are inappropriate to the occasion, this is a choice you are making. It is your decision and not due to fate or the fault of someone or some-thing else.

Think, again, of the "craziest" person you've ever met. What is her problem? The problem, of course, is that her thinking is wrong (i.e. faulty, illogical, "out of touch with reality," so to speak). And how can she be helped? Only by helping her change her thinking to a more logical, rational position. This process may occur rapidly or more slowly depending upon how "lost" she is, and upon the extent to which she wants (or does not want) to change. A third option is that she may simply choose to remain in the world she has "created" rather than return to the one she left.

2. How Clara Went Crazy

When I was a child there was a woman in the community whom everyone said was crazy. I never doubted it for a moment. As far as anyone knew she had been a normal, healthy, caring and responsible lady who simply "went crazy." It was during World War II and her son was sent overseas to fight. Those who seemed to know "the rest of the story" said she worried about her son's safety to the point that she "lost her mind." She apparently couldn't stand the thought of living day after day wondering if someone in an army uniform would come to tell her that her boy (as she always referred to him) was dead or missing in action. The constant anticipation of receiving bad news (her negative thought process) became a daily habit, a way of life that gradually became real. I think she decided to go ahead and kill her boy in her mind and get it over with. She must have decided that it was bound to happen anyway. It was perhaps easier for her to live with the thought of her son being dead than to constantly wonder and have to finally deal with the reality should it occur. So, she chose to live in a world where he was dead; a world of hurt and grief, but at least a world more constant than the previous one where she never knew for sure, and didn't want to know in case the news was bad. When the war ended and her son came home unharmed she never accepted him. She saw him as an imposter because her boy died in the war. Here was a perfectly normal (as far as anyone knew) woman who chose to live in another world, a world she could never manage to escape. Her thinking never changed back to reality.

You can create another world because, for whatever reason, you don't want to live in the present (real?) world. Eventually you convince yourself that the created world is the real one. You get "set" into it and become at home with it. You may choose to stay there for a while or for the rest of your life. If the created (imagined?) world becomes more threatening and awful than the "real" world you may choose to return. Coming and going may give the impression after a while that both worlds exist and you can go and come whenever you please. This is probably worse than living permanently in one or the other. It might also give the false impression that there are two personalities involved. What is called "mental illness" is a process of changing one's mind from a rational position to an irrational, fractured, untenable one.

"Mental health" is another wrong term, in the same sense that "mental illness" is the wrong term. Mental health, if it means anything, can only refer to a pattern of dealing with reality (i.e. daily living, decisions, behavior) logically and consistently so that good decisions/choices are made with a reasonable understanding of possible consequences. So much of what is called therapy deals with issues unrelated to the thinking process. For example: A building is on fire. So do you talk with the people in the building about types of fires, how each one feels about fires, dangers and precautions; or do you try to understand the immediacy of the situation (event), and devise an immediate and effective method of extinguishing the fire and/or evacuating the building? My point is that therapy often involves talking about feelings/emotions but never gets around to helping individuals change faulty thinking (i.e. putting out the fire).

3. The Emperor is Naked

Hans Christian Anderson wrote the classic story, *The Emperor's New Clothes.* Everyone knew all along that the emperor had no clothes on, but no one would admit it for fear of appearing foolish or of being different from everyone else. A child finally told the simply truth which freed the others to admit the truth also—the emperor has no clothes! Somewhere along the way we need to come to terms with the business of "mental illness" and "mental health." The two-sided coin of mental illness/mental health is, at worst fiction, and at best wrong terminology.

4. Mental Incompetence

It could be argued that anyone (everyone) who commits a crime, say of murder, must have been "mentally ill" at the time of the crime, at least for a while, otherwise the person would not have committed the crime. After all, no person in his right mind would ever have done such a thing. Thus, no one should ever be found guilty of any crime.

What is the problem? Something is terribly wrong with this picture. Either the criminal justice system convicted some poor, unfortunate souls who are victims because they couldn't help what they did (they were mentally ill, therefore mentally incompetent to stand trial and cannot be convicted), or the idea of deciding that a criminal is mentally incompetent to stand trial by evaluating the answers to some questions is blatantly absurd. If an individual is competent to (chose to) commit a crime, that individual, by the same sort of reasoning, is most certainly competent to stand trial. My point is that if there is no "mental illness," then the idea of being incompetent to stand trial makes no sense. The only way it makes sense is if an individual had a physical problem such as retardation.

Just because an individual chooses to think irrationally and to act illegally does not mean that he is incompetent to stand trial. In what sense is he incompetent? He can answer questions. He can make statements. He obviously can make decisions. He is liable for his actions. In fact, he must stand trial. How else can a legal opinion by a judge and jury be reached? Giving the "wrong" (or right if he is sly) answers to some questions does not prove that an individual is incompetent to stand trial. Deciding that an individual is incompetent to face up to his crime based upon an interview wherein the individual gives skewed, irrational responses to questions and who talks and acts "crazy" is not a basis for not allowing the trial to take its normal, usual course.

Courts sometimes find defendants who commit crimes not guilty by reason of insanity (GBMI, guilty but mentally ill) apparently because they find it too difficult to believe that anyone in her right mind would have committed a particular crime. In other words, one would have to be crazy or insane (or whatever term one wishes to use) in order to commit a heinous deed. Of course, juries are not always persuaded by the so-called insanity argument. For example, a woman from Texas who drowned her five children was found guilty and given a life sentence. The defense argued that the defendant didn't really know right from wrong at the time she committed the crime. The prosecution argued that she knew precisely what she was doing. In fact, immediately after the crimes were committed the defendant called her husband to tell him he needed to come home, and then she called the police to report what she had done. Although some "reasons" were given by "mental health experts" as to why she did what she did the jury simply didn't buy it.

Suppose the jury had found the defendant innocent by reason of insanity. Several problems would immediately have arisen. First, how could a psychologist, the jury, the judge or anyone else possibly know her reasons for killing her children? The reasons given were that she was trying to save them from going to hell (or something to that effect), that she suffered from postpartum depression, and that she had previously been hospitalized for depression. And this was supposed to excuse the fact that she committed five murders! The first reason is beyond ridiculous (How does this sound? Hello, Police. I just killed my children in order to save them, but I really didn't know what I was doing.) The second is questionable (i.e. there apparently is a question as to whether there is even such an "illness" as postpartum depression. And even if there is a connection between such an illness and the fact that she killed her children it does not appear clear and convincing.) The third reason, that she had a history of depression, is not a valid reason to find her not guilty. Simply because a psychologist or therapist suggests that someone is not capable of standing trial and should not be found guilty because they are "mentally incompetent" does not mean that it is a fact. It is a subjective opinion.

So, suppose you had been on the jury in this case and the woman was found innocent. And what if a few years later this same woman drowned another child, her own or a neighbor's. In order to be consistent the court would be compelled to, once again, find her not guilty for the same reasons that were given in the first trial. Then, what if a hundred women decided to drown their children and offer some ridiculous claim (God, voices, and so forth, told them to; they were really trying to save their children from some future evil; they were depressed; or whatever), how would the court respond? Based on the reasoning of the defense counsel and testimony from "expert" witnesses, all would be found innocent by reason of insanity. Actually, faulty thinking produces inappropriate emotions and inappropriate actions. What one does (behavior) is always a choice. A person should be judged by a court of law based upon what he or she did, not upon some subjective opinion as to the perceived or supposed thinking or mental state of the person at the time. Any act must be preceded by the thought (the decision) to do it.

5. How David Feigned Insanity

Feigning craziness is not a new tactic for fooling courts of law. There is an interesting, if somewhat strange, story in the Old Testament (1 Samuel 21:13f) about David playing crazy in order to save himself from his enemies. David was running from King Saul (who was himself something of a mad man and very jealous of David). David went to Gath where a person named Achish was "king" (he wasn't actually a king but something like a captain or warlord, but that's incidental to the story). When David and his party arrived, David was recognized by some of Achish's people who pointed out that he was the person who had killed goliath the Philistine and he was even carrying Goliath's sword. David became afraid of what Achish might do to him. So, in order to get himself out of what looked like a precarious situation, he thought of a plan that just might work: he would pretend to be crazy, to feign madness. Verse 13 is rather specific and descriptive of David's actions: "He changed his behavior before them; he pretended to be mad when in their presence. He scratched marks on the doors of the gate, and let his spittle run down his beard." He must have been a pretty good actor because Achish was convinced that David was crazy and he decided to have nothing to do with him. He said to his assistants, "Don't I have enough crazy people around me without you bringing me another? Get him out of my house." That, of course, was David's plan and it worked perfectly. One is reminded of briar rabbit who begged not to be thrown into the briar patch which is exactly where he wanted to be. The key point in this story is that David "changed his behavior before them, and pretended (or feigned) madness." He did it deliberately, as a tactic for survival. He was not crazy, but he acted crazy until he "departed from there and escaped to the cave of Adullam" where he was joined by family, friends and supporters.

Since ancient times crazy people (lunatics, the "insane," individuals thought to be extremely foolish) have been regarded with special awe because they were believed to be possessed by spirits (see *Interpreter's Bible*, Vol. 2, p. 999). This belief is evident in a book (and movie) about a white girl who was captured by Indians. She survived because they thought she was possessed or "touched" by the spirits. It has probably been out of a combination of sympathy and fear that people have never known exactly how to deal with such individuals, so they simply leave them alone.

A recent example of a person who appears to fit the David model is the man from Utah who kidnapped a teen-age girl for the alleged purpose of forcing her to become his wife. At his trial he was declared "mentally incompetent to stand trial." The judge ruled that he be sent to a state hospital until he is deemed capable to stand trial. According to a newspaper report the defendant repeatedly shouted biblical admonitions and sang hymns during the hearing which prompted him to be removed from the courtroom several times. Testimony was also given that his family had a history of "mental disorders." So, look at the pattern: The defendant is "mentally incompetent" to stand trial; he is sent to a hospital (as though he has a physical problem of some sort); he shouts and sings and appears "crazy" in the courtroom; and, alas, his family (pretty vague as to who this includes) has a history of "mental disorders." (One could write a doctoral dissertation on the problems related to this trial.) For example: What is the basis for the determination that someone is "mentally incompetent to stand trial? As has been suggested previously, such judgment is highly subjective and based largely upon unwarranted assumptions. And why would the defendant in this case be sent to a hospital? A hospital suggests a physical problem. Also, the fact that the defendant appears to be (acts) crazy does not mean he is crazy. And even if he is, in fact, crazy (i.e. his thoughts, emotions and behavior are illogical, irrational), he is still guilty of a felony. And last, what does the fact that the defendant came from what might be called a dysfunctional family have to do with his decision (his plan, his choice) to kidnap someone? Any attempt at a connection would be a stretch since the defendant, himself, chose his actions.

The outcome of this trial is nothing short of amazingly absurd. But, the tactics worked. The village chief let David, the future king of Israel, get away with feigning madness. A man in Utah was declared incompetent to stand trial. It's a ploy that has obviously been working for as long as history has been recorded. It's one of humanity's oldest tricks, but it still works. And as long as voodoo thinking continues to influence and convince lawyers, judges and juries such ridiculous approaches to justice will continue to find their way into courtrooms.

The problem with craziness, it seems to me, is twofold. First, how can you determine if someone is feigning madness? There appears to be a fundamental difference between someone who pretends to be crazy in order to get out of a serious situation and someone who has actually decided to leave the world of reality and live in a world of his own creation, a world of craziness. At the same time, the thought process (for example, the decision to commit a crime, for whatever reason) is the same. The intention was to commit the crime. Second, when it comes to the justice system does it really make any difference? Should individuals not be judged on the basis of their actual deeds (actions) and not on the basis of their assumed state of mind? I believe the intention is the same. If you committed a crime and you pretended to be crazy (insane) at the time; or if you committed the crime during such time as you were (or are) "crazy" (i.e. you were living in a world of non-reality, but which you chose to create and live in), how would a court of law be able to determine the difference? The criminal could answer the therapist's or lawyer's questions in such a way that they could never know with certainty. There is no test that could with one hundred percent accuracy determine the difference. Therefore, the only rational method of dealing with any crime committed is to conduct the trial and reach a verdict based solely on the evidence presented.

It seems to me that madness/craziness/insanity can be accomplished in one of two ways. First, by design (i.e. by plan, intentionally, in order to temporarily escape or avoid responsibility/accountability or an unpleasant/bad/dangerous situation) which is what David did. In such cases most individuals "return" to reality when the crisis is over because they never really left to begin with. They simply used non-reality for convenience. Second, some choose madness to escape/avoid a highly unpleasant, seemingly unbearable and unpredictable situation, which is what Clara did. (Examples might include long term abuse, extreme physical pain or hunger, trying to survive in a war-ravaged area, extreme and unexpected personal loss or natural disasters, and so on.) In these kinds of situations one may or may not return to reality. It depends upon a number of factors: the intensity of the perceived situation (threat against oneself), how strong and embedded beliefs about the situation are, and how easy it is to live in the newly created world of illusion. In either case responsibility and accountability must be considered. To fail to hold people responsible/accountable only exacerbates the notion of "mental illness" and contributes to the design and acceptance of an untrue, unreal world.

6. Hearing Voices

I recall talking with a man who told me that he heard voices which told him to do certain things (usually violent and/or illegal things), and he asked me how I accounted for it. He stated that the voices are audible (i.e. as though coming from a hidden speaker and not just in his mind). Now, from this short piece of information what can I reasonably conclude?

First, I cannot account for his statement that he hears voices. It is he who says he hears voices. This is not part of my experience. I do not hear voices from someone who isn't there and, quite frankly, I do not believe he does either. Just because he claims to hear voices does not mean that he actually hears voices.

Second, I believe the "voices" are in his mind; that is, his own thoughts, part of his own experience. Whatever is happening it is part of his world, real or imagined. Therefore, he should treat the "voices" as he would treat any other kind of information he receives. He should analyze, critique and evaluate (A.C.E.) it. Is it correct? Does it make sense? Is it good, trustworthy information? And, especially, what would likely be the results of doing what the voice(s) suggested?

Third, he can do with the information he receives (hears) whatever he wants. It is his choice whether to accept it as accurate, valid and trustworthy and whether to act on it. The information is part of his world; it is part of his thinking, along with other thoughts. (It seems strange that the "voices" always tell him to do something bad, never something good.)

Fourth, he is responsible, ultimately, regarding how to handle/process the "voices" (i.e. the information he receives). I doubt that he does everything else he is told to do, or that he follows through on every other suggestion that is made to him. So why should he believe these particular voices, especially if the voices suggest a violent, immoral or illegal act? If I (or any real person) told him that he ought to go down the street and rob a bank I doubt that he would take that as good advice or as an order from someone he had better obey and, therefore, go rob the bank. In other words, why would he listen to a "voice" that he does not actually hear or verify? He admitted that the voices he claimed to hear could not be tape recorded, so they weren't real in the sense that he heard my voice and could tape record it. In short, why should he obey the voices? The answer of course is that he doesn't have to. If he obeys the voices it is because he chooses to, which is the same as saying that he is going to do what he wants and the voice is a convenient excuse. Whatever he does, voice or no voice, he is responsible.

Fifth, determining that this man has a "mental illness" and attempting to deal with on that basis would be as ridiculous as believing that he hears voices in the first place. To begin with, how could it ever be proven that he in fact does (or for that matter, does not) hear voices? It can only be said that the chances of hearing voices without a live human being or a mechanical agency producing the voices is nil to nothing based on normal, everyday experience. The only "treatment" that would be effective would be to try to convince him that his thinking is faulty, that people do not actually hear voices from people who aren't physically present, and that the "voices" are actually his own thoughts.

Sixth, this man saying he hears voices is not really the main issue. The question is, is he responsible for his actions? I believe he is. If he says that God or Jesus or some other religious figure spoke to him he should still be challenged regarding whether God or Jesus or other religious figure would actually want him to hurt himself or someone else or to commit a crime. If God is love (and love means acting in your own or someone else's best interest) then it would be inconsistent for God to suggest a harmful act. In other words, the validity of the voice should be questioned. In any case, whatever the voice is and whatever he decides to do, he is ultimately responsible and will have to pay whatever consequences are called for. As I said earlier, hearing voices is not the issue. There is really nothing all that unusual about "hearing voices." People have heard voices (reflection, contemplation, weighing of issues) as far back as recorded history. The real issue is that you had better decide which voices you are going to listen to and be influenced by.

D. Emotion

1. A River of Emotion

It's impossible to listen to the news on the radio or T.V., read the newspaper or even watch a sports event on television without being bombarded with the words "emotion and emotional." These words are used ad nauseam. Look at the following examples: emotional day, emotional encounter, emotional case (i.e. court case), emotional meeting, emotional response, emotional game, emotional reunion, emotional fatigue, emotional energy, emotional interview, emotional disturbance, emotional illness, emotional I.Q., emotional moment, emotional leader, the air was filled with emotion, and so on. A woman being interview on a T.V. news documentary stated, in response to a particular question, that her decision was "an emotional decision, not an intellectual one."

What does emotion(al) mean? Why is it so hard to define or even to discuss emotion? It is, in fact, an extremely complex subject. A workable, defensible definition (at least one that most everyone is likely to agree on) is highly unlikely for a number of reasons, the major one perhaps being that the various academic disciplines tend to be episteme centric. In other words, psychologists are from Venus, sociologists are from Mars, and philosophers are inter-planetary. There is nothing wrong with various disciplines offering their own unique perspectives, of course, as long as they don't take a cave type mentality that refuses to consider other avenues and possibilities.

One problem is that while emotion and emotional are widely used words, they are often used in unclear, ambiguous and inappropriate ways. When a sports announcer says that a particular athlete is playing with emotion, what exactly is he talking about? What are you supposed to know from having heard that remark? Is the athlete happy or sad? Laughing or crying? Angry or embarrassed? Excited or upset? "Emotional" can refer to an extremely wide range of meanings, either positive or negative. So, what is going on in all those situations where "emotion" or "emotional" is used? To say that someone (or some-thing, which is even worse) is emotional is non-descriptive. It tells little or nothing about what is or was actually happening. It's like the meteor-ologists saying that we're having weather. The most obvious problem with the use (and misuse) of the terms "emotion/emotional" is the tendency to assume a disconnect between thinking and emotions.

To use emotion in such a generic sense ignores the thinking and behavioral aspects. It is impossible to consider emotion without first considering the thinking that produced it; and second, the action which demonstrated it. Even then, trying to describe various emotions (i.e. giving emotions labels, names) assumes that such emotions actually exist. For example, how does one "look" angry? Actually, you may look a certain way without feeling or sensing anger. You may, in fact, have a headache. Behavior should be described in more detailed, accurate terms than simply "emotional."

Other than assigning labels to emotions (and there seems to be no limit to the number of them), emotion is extremely difficult to define. Yet, it is important to have some understanding of what emotion is and how emotion is related to thought and behavior. One reason for the difficulty relates to the perennial mind-body problem (about which more is said in another section). To say that emotion is feeling is like saying water is wet. The usual dictionary definition of emotion is "intense feeling" which is basically like saying water is very wet. Psychology text books often refer to emotion as patterns of arousal. I'm not sure what that means. Perhaps it means that emotion is a physical reaction to specific patterns of thought; that emotion is thought manifest; that it is the way you interpret and deal with the environment; or a response to intellectual stimuli. Perhaps.

I wonder if it is possible to ever be non-emotional. Or, to put it another way, is emotion something that can be turned on and off? An analogy (though perhaps not the best one) might be that an engine, while running, may be just idling. The idea is that emotion is always "on" but not always obvious or observable. Most event evaluation produces no recognizable emotion because most events are routine, expected and easily evaluated (i.e. interpreted or classified). Otherwise, emotions that are obvious and observable (i.e. physically manifest) are either positive or negative depending upon the evaluation of events. When a statement is made that someone or something is emotional the reference is usually about observable negative emotions. If someone cries she may be said to be emotional. But if she laughs her behavior is not usually said to be emotional. This distinction is cause for further confusion regarding an understanding of emotion.

The Latin word "emovere" means to move out. The Hindu idea of emotion is "rasa," or juice/extract/flavor. These types of definitions describe emotion in terms of social situations instead of feelings. The metaphor is taste and nourishment instead of the Western notion or venting or letting off steam.

Emotions can be thought of somewhat like the various shades of colors. For example, there are any number of synonyms for anger just as there are many shades of red. There are several synonyms for depression just as there are a number of shades of blue. There are various synonyms for envy just as there are several shades of green. And there must be a dozen synonyms for happiness just as there are an equal number of shades of yellow. Trying to identify and focus on all manner of emotions misses the point. Emotions are basically either positive or negative. Sometimes it is virtually impossible, even futile, to try to label emotions. For example, how is frustration or disgust or being "fed up" different from anger (anger, in this case, defined as "misplaced aggression")? I believe that at the root of all negative emotions is anger. And there is no point in discussing positive emotions at this point because they apparently pose no problem. I have never heard of anyone seeking counseling for being simply too happy. Anger, like all negative emotions (whatever their labels) that result in inappropriate behavior, is preceded by faulty thinking. The focus should always be on thinking, not on emotions or behavior. So, don't concentrate on how you feel. In the final analysis, it really doesn't matter how you feel about anything. Feeling does not get the job done. Feeling, like happiness and self-esteem, is always a by-product. Concentrate on accurate, logical, mature thinking. The rest will follow.

In a sense emotion can be thought of as the energy needed to carry out various actions (behavior). The so-called fight or flight stance is an example of how this might work. If an event is evaluated (interpreted) as fearful or dangerous, the body functions in a certain manner to deal successfully with the real or perceived threat or danger. However, nothing happens until thinking occurs. The body doesn't fight or flee until the mind decides what to do. Neither emotion nor action precedes thought. Even though emotion is a physical reaction, thought is always primary.

In spite of the difficulty with trying to formulate a definition of emotion, I think there are some ways of thinking about emotion that can be helpful. Emotion involves a highly complex set of tools (method may be a better word) for self-preservation; how you preserve or conduct yourself (i.e. exist, carry on, maintain yourself) in view of what is taking place around you (which I simply call events). Emotion places thinking and acting on the same level. If thinking and acting are on different levels, then the thought would not necessarily justify the action. Emotion is an attempt to justify (or rectify) action. I say attempt because the evaluation of a particular event may not be logical (i.e. accurate, reasonable) which, consequently, would lead to an inappropriate emotion and (assuming that action is followed) an inappropriate action. You may be angry enough to hit another person but not follow through with the action (actually hitting the person) because another notion comes into play, the notion of possible negative sanctions.

I read in a philosophy magazine that "people's beliefs are very often swayed by their emotions." Coming from a well known philosopher I was surprised at this statement. I believe just the opposite is true, that people's emotions are swayed (actually caused) by their beliefs. How is it possible that emotions (which are created by belief, by thinking in the first place) can sway or influence belief? This would be like being convicted of a crime even before the crime was committed. In understanding the relationship of event, evaluation and emotion, sequence is important. It is always T.E.A. - thinking, emotion, and then action (behavior), never in any other order (e.g. not E.A.T., E.T.A., A.T.E. or A.E.T.). T.E.A. occurs so rapidly that it is virtually simultaneous, as a single operation. It is easy to assume that emotions or actions occur first. Have you ever said, "If I had just thought, I wouldn't have done thus or so?" But you did think. And that's the point. Beliefs (thinking) cannot be swayed by emotion or action. After a particular action, you may be surprised at your action. But, then, you had to think about it in order to be surprised. Thinking to some degree and on some level must occur or nothing else can happen.

Emotion is created (in a sense crafted) in the mind based upon how events are evaluated, and why events are evaluated as they are. A higher premium is placed upon certain events than on others. Any term used to described an emotion is actually a social construct that follows a certain pattern which is based upon factors such as perception, acculturation and self-preservation. Actual emotion is the result/product of evaluation, positive or negative. And there is no limit to the names that can be given to this process. Did you ever try to make a list of all the negative and positive emotions? The list will be as long as your imagination will permit.

Emotion is sometimes based upon a sense of expectation. A sports announcer, prior to a game that has been given a lot of media attention and has a long established rivalry, might say something like: "You can feel the emotion in the air." He says this because he expects that the fans will shout encouraging words, boo the referee, wave their arms and clap their hands; in other words, they will do all the things fans usually do. The announcer refers to these sounds and actions collectively as emotion. But can he actually "feel" it? He, himself, is (by his own use of the term) being "emotional." T.V. interviewers often insist on the emotional moment. They ask, "How did you feel when this or that happened?" Or, "describe your emotion at the time." Emotion is much overrated; thinking is much underrated.

"Feel" is not a synonym for "think." "Feel" is often used when "think" would be more appropriate. Emotion is often used as though emotion exists apart, separate from thought; as though emotions have a life of their own and simply float around waiting to land up some unsuspecting person and wreak all kinds of havoc. For some reason our society seems to prefer using the word "emotion" and/or "emotional" instead of terms that actually describe behavior. Maybe it's because we've gotten away from being specific about practically everything. We seem to like generalities, vagueness and language that lacks precision and clarity. So, instead of saying someone is happy or sad or whatever, we are more inclined to simply say he is emotional. It avoids the details of having to figure out where emotions come from to begin with.

Following the 9-11-01 terrorist incident a woman said, "I feel so emotional about those who lost loved ones in the explosions." Granted that was a humane statement and the woman should be commended for caring. But that isn't the point. The point is, why not say I feel sorry, frustrated, angry, sad (or whatever) for the families who lost loved ones instead of using the generic, virtually meaningless term emotional? No one knows for sure how the woman felt (you have to imagine), just that she felt something emotional. Actually, to use the term emotional as a substitute for descriptive terminology does much to trivialize, minimize and reduce the significance of genuine feelings.

Consider the following three situations (events): In the morning you attend a funeral of someone you knew well.

You become "emotional." In the afternoon you attend a wedding of one of your best friends. You become "emotional." Then, in the evening you attend a ball game and root for your favorite team. You become "emotional." Now, what were you doing at these three events? In what sense were you "emotional?" It would make little sense to simply use the generic term "emotional" to describe your feelings in all three, very different, situations. However, if you said you were sad, happy and excited; or you felt grief, joy and exuberance; that would make more sense. Such language would be a more accurate assessment of your emotions than to just say you were emotional. Obviously, your thinking (evaluation of each event) led to your various emotions related to the three events.

It is important to understand that thoughts have no existence apart from the brain, no life of their own, so to speak. And in similar fashion emotions have no existence apart from thought. An analogy might be that a shadow cannot exist by itself, apart from the body which casts it. You cannot "act on emotion" (an expression I hear often), you emote upon thinking; and only then do you act if, in fact, you choose to act at all. You cannot become angry or happy whether you want to or not. Emotions must have consent. You are not compelled to choose any particular emotion or to act in a prescribed manner. Emotion and action are deliberate choices arrived at through thinking.

It is a truism that behavior is learned. Instinct in human beings can hardly be said to exist any more, at least on a purely animal level. Human beings were weaned of anything that might be termed instinct long ago. (This statement can, of course, be argued.) Emotions are basically learned also. You learn to respond differently in different situations depending upon the manner in which you have been socialized. You will exhibit certain emotions relating to your sense of physical well-being and your sense of survival (e.g. the fear of falling from a high place or being injured or killed in the presence of a grizzly bear). You also learn and evoke certain "social" emotions (e.g. you feel hurt if a friend says something which you evaluate as untrue, unkind or rude).

Why do emotions change? If you are angry why don't you remain in an angry state? How do you cease being angry and then become happy (or exhibit some other emotion)? How do you change from one emotion to another, often in a short space of time? Emotions change, obviously, because thoughts change. You do not stay angry, or happy or sad or excited because your thoughts do not stay the same. Theoretically, it would seem that if your thoughts remained the same, then your corresponding emotion would remain the same. Thankfully, both change.

2. Damaged Emotions

Language/terminology is usually a major problem in any area, with any operation and in any setting. Terminology relating to emotion is a major problem and a primary source of confusion. For example, a term that is used a lot but hardly challenged is "damaged emotions." On the surface it sounds like an accurate medical term; but underneath the surface it is actually another example of absurd terminology. How is it logically possible for an emotion (or a group of emotions) to be or become damaged? You can exhibit or describe an emotion, but how can that particular emotion become damaged? There is no evidence that damaged emotions exist, let alone that there is some kind of cure for them. Yet, large sums of money are sometimes "awarded" by courts of law to "victims" of "mental suffering and anguish." People often accept such terminology without much question. But a seconds worth of thought should reveal that it is inaccurate and illogical.

A local T.V. reporter was interviewing a bright high school senior. Referring to one of his teachers, the reporter asked the student, "How does she make you feel?" The student, appearing somewhat perplexed, replied, "She doesn't make me feel anything." I gave that student an "A." He gave a good answer to a bad question. The problem is that this is typical of many of the questions that reporters, as well as others, ask. Such questions attempt to elicit an "emotional" response.

3. Levels of Events, Evaluation, Emotions and Actions

I suggest that there is a corresponding connection between event, evaluation, emotion and action, and that this connection may be thought of in terms of levels. For example:

Levels of events, evaluation and emotion: Level I - Routine, mundane, predictable, acceptable, obvious, no questions, no problem. Level II - Annoyance, frustration, somewhat questionable but barely a problem. Level III - Unexpected (but not unknown), personal, maybe threatening, may involve legal or formal resolution, interruption, unpleasant, definitely a problem. Level IV - Major trauma, crisis, unexpected, unanticipated (but not necessarily totally unknown or unheard of), requires some serious adjustment and/or reallocation of resources, may be multi-dimensional, affective, no immediate solution, major disruption or disturbance, possibly very costly personally as well as economically. Level V - Terrible, catastrophic (e.g. 9-11-01, natural disaster of major proportions), anything effecting large areas and/or numbers, totally unexpected, shocking, major disorientation, no immediate or future solution or adjustment in sight, very long term.

Connections: Levels of events correspond directly and proportionally with levels of evaluations and then with emotional levels. Evaluations are basically interpretations of perceived data. As events occur they are immediately processed by the mind into various levels or categories based in part upon prior response patterns. The key is that event, evaluation and emotion should be on the same or corresponding level simultaneously.

As an example of how the levels might operate, consider the events of 9-11-01. This event would be viewed (at least by most Americans) at the highest level (Level V) because of several factors at work at the same time (a syndrome, if you will). Namely:

1) The quantity of people killed, well over 2000 seems enormous compared to one or even several. An airplane crash would be seen as extremely serious; but dealing with almost 3000, and in the manner in which they were killed, was almost beyond comprehension for many.

2) The fact that there were four major catastrophes in the space of a few minutes gave little time to fully grasp, evaluate or process what happened as compared with the more "usual" bad events.

3) The result/effect: Event, evaluation and emotion (and action if action is required) should be on the same level.

Emotional levels occur in conjunction with perceived levels of events followed by a certain course of action. Emotion is always connected to experience (past), perception (present) and anticipation (future). Emotion is also connected to value judgments (which correspond to the levels discussed above) of appearances which, of course, may or may not represent reality. Once you make a judgment (i.e. evaluate an event in a certain way) then you will also act in a certain way, on the same level if both emotion and action are appropriate in relation to the event or events.

Martha C. Nussbaum, in *Upheavals of Thought: The Intelligence of Emotions*, states that "emotions are inherently cognitive operations which involve judgments about important things; and those judgments become emotional precisely by their connection to the emoter's neediness. That is, things matter only when they affect us directly. Only then do they elicit an emotional reaction. All emotions are egocentric." Emotions are vehicles which "attach" to and give impetus to thought. Thought cannot in/of/by itself do or produce anything. Mind cannot move or effect matter. Emotion is the dynamic aspect that "moves" the body to complete evaluations/decisions in a particular manner.

Some psychologists theorize about why we remember some things and don't remember other things. That is, why do we remember a tornado but can't remember where we parked the car? They attach the answer to emotions. They contend that we remember things we are "highly emotional" about. But why do we become "highly emotional" in the first place? I think it is because of the evaluation (interpretation, assessment) phase which involves levels (or rankings, if you will). Parking the car (Level I) can become so routine that it has little significance in comparison with a tornado (Level IV or V depending on its severity and outcome). A tornado will likely be "highly emotional" because it will normally be thought of as highly significant. If a tornado is viewed as Level V, it will normally be followed (immediately, instantly) by Level V emotion and, most likely, Level V action. The problem occurs, of course, when the levels do not correspond, which may happen due to faulty thinking/assessment, insufficient information or knowledge, or simply a naïve or immature view of the situation as a whole. For example, inconsistent levels might look like this:

Event - Severe hurricane warning is issued (Level IV or V).

Evaluation - You took it lightly. You're going to ride it out. You've never experienced a hurricane before so it might be interesting (Level II, maybe III).

Emotion - You aren't too worried nor apparently afraid (Level II).

The problem is that the levels do not correspond. Given the above scenario the event, evaluation, emotion and action should all be, say, Level IV. If the levels are IV, III and II then there is the potential for a problem of some proportion. A major problem occurs when, for example, a level I event is evaluated as a higher level and the corresponding action is also in the same higher level. Of course, it can work in the opposite way also. A level IV, for example, can be taken too lightly and evaluated as a level I or II. The point is that everything should be level appropriate.

4. Mind-Body Connection

Emotion may be thought of as the connection (at least as much of a connection as there is likely to be) between mind and body. Without an emotional component all events, thoughts (i.e. decisions, choices) and actions (behavior) would be of equal value (i.e. on the same level). There would be no need for moral or ethical distinctions, balancing, discerning, and so forth. It is natural and normal for human beings to classify, categorize, organize and prioritize. Emotion serves the purpose of typing, classifying, judging and harmonizing thought with action (or, at least, perceived action). Thought plus emotion fortunately does not always translate into or reach the point of action. Emotion may be compared to cocking the trigger and pointing the gun but not always firing. For most of us, if we actually did everything we thought about doing, not only would we be liable to spend a good portion of our lives in jail, society itself would become so chaotic it would lead to a persistent state of anomie. So, emotion involves thought plus perceived purpose transferred into action.

Emotion involves the level of importance associated with events. Some events are so routine as to elicit virtually no emotion, while other events may rank higher on the scale. Emotion is always relative, always comparative to something else. The difference/disparity determines the level of the emotion. Emotion is obviously judgmental. That's its job. Emotions have objects (i.e. emotions are directional and specific). You are angry AT someone, ABOUT something. You are sad because of some event or remembrance of the event. There must be a reason for a particular emotion. The reason may or may not be logical or justified. Furthermore, it may be determined after the fact that the original "reason" was not reasonable/logical. If beauty is in the eye of the beholder, emotion is in the mind of the believer.

5. Emotion and Choice

Emotions are choices made, not verdicts handed down. Emotions are crosses to be carried, not burdens to be bourn. Emotions are chosen as a result of how events are evaluated. You are not stuck with any particular emotion about any particular event. Emotions are not legislated or pre-packaged or pre-scripted for market (mind) consumption. Emotion does not operate like a physical law (E=MC2; water freezes at 32°F; two objects of different size fall at the same rate of speed; light travels at 186,000 miles per second). In one sense emotion is whatever you want it to be. You may choose to become extremely angry, moderately angry, merely annoyed or ignore a particular event altogether. There is no rule or law that determines or dictates your choice or level of emotion. There may be a precedent for such emotion. That is, you may have witnessed the emotional reactions (emotion plus action) of others in similar situations and simply imitated the "expected" response. But, in any case, you feel however you choose to feel. It would be much easier if each event you didn't like or agree with had a corresponding emotional instruction with it. There would be an appropriate, pre-packaged, pre-conditioned emotion to fit every occasion. But as it is you choose, and sometimes your choices turn out to be inappropriate and hard to live with.

Viktor E. Frankl, a Viennese psychotherapist, survived Auschwitz, but his mother, brother and pregnant wife were killed by the Nazis. He lost everything dear to himself except one thing: "the last of human freedoms: to choose one's attitude in any given set of circumstances." Frankl doesn't specifically use the term "emotion/feeling" but the idea seems to be the same. Emotion (attitude) is actually a choice; and choice is truly awesome because it places responsibility squarely on the back of each individual. The existential element is both haunting and humbling.

Placing emotion within the context of choice seems too simplistic for many. But there's no other logical way to view it. Again, the perennial language problem arises. Statements such as "I let my emotions take over," "she became emotional," and "his emotions were damaged," are some examples. In a review of Daniel Goleman's book entitled *Emotional Intelligence*, the writer stated that the book "offers specific steps for nurturing and strengthening emotional skills." If you blink you might jump right over the notion that there may be a problem here. The very idea of an "emotional skill" is baffling. The title of the book itself begs for logical explanation. Even if emotion could be separated from thought, how could a criteria be constructed to measure it or to determine that one emotion is more "intelligent" than another? This is an excellent example of the proverbial cart and horse problem. (Or even worse, the ghost outside the body.) Talking about intelligence is one thing; emotional intelligence is quite another.

An article by David Schepp entitled *Heart of the Matter* (Courier-Journal, Louisville, Kentucky, May 12, 2003) listed sixteen questions that are supposed to help you determine your E.Q. ("emotional intelligence"). The problem is the same. Emotions cannot be thought of, talked about, managed with (or without) skill, or examined, or ranked or anything else apart from thought. The idea that an emotion (any particular emotion, or the idea of emotion itself) can have intelligence seems preposterous. Emotion cannot be a separate category apart from thought anymore than a mind can get along without a body.

Emotions change as thoughts change. Suppose you are a college student away from home and you receive a letter in the mail telling you that your uncle Frank died. Depending upon your relationship with and your perception and memory of your uncle, you may have a variety of simultaneous emotions (probably sadness, grief) based upon your evaluation of this event. You may think (evaluate) something like: Uncle Frank used to take me fishing, always remembered my birthday, had a great sense of humor, and so on. So, you feel sad at the news of his death. But, then, the letter goes on to say that Uncle Frank left you $50,000 in his will. Now your evaluation (thought process) may change somewhat. You may still be sad, but you also begin to process the idea of having $50,000 and what you can do with it. You may go from sadness to elation and back and forth. The evaluation process can involve a wide range of thoughts and emotions. But the point is, your emotions change as your thoughts change, which is to say that thinking creates emotions. "Mixed emotions" result from "mixed" thinking.

6. Head vs. Heart

A young woman in a discussion group said that her head told her one thing and her heart told her another. She was in love with a man from England and he wanted them to be married and live in London. That he might stay in the United States was apparently not an option. While she said she loved him and wanted them to be married, she wasn't sure she was willing to leave her family, her city, her surroundings and move to another country. She said her heart was telling her one thing (marry and move to London) and her head was telling her something else (i.e. I really don't want to move to London). As the discussion continued it became evident that this woman was simply trying to choose between two apparently equally desirable alternatives. She had a clear choice to make: marry the man she loved and move to

England or not marry and stay where she was.

Actually this woman didn't have a head vs. heart problem at all. She had, in fact, a head vs. head problem. She needed to make a choice between something she wanted to do and something she thought she ought to do. After she weighed all the pros and cons she could come up with, she decided that her country, her family, her city and her way of life were more important to her than marrying the man she was in love with.

In logical terms this kind of decision making may be referred to as breaking the horns of a dilemma. The dilemma is that you can't have it both ways. You have a choice, a decision. Both marrying and moving away and not marrying and staying at home were not possibilities. Making the best choice possible, one she could most comfortably live with, was the only solution. You make the choice, and then you live with it; you live by the consequences of your decisions.

You don't have an emotional heart and a rational head. You don't think and make choices with your heart, so forget about your heart. Again, it's a matter of using appropriate language. Referring to the heart may be a poetic or romantic notion but it has nothing to do with logic. Choices are always between two or more alternatives; sometimes between "evils," and sometimes between equally desirable "goods." But it's always a head vs. head problem. Trying to think in terms of head vs. heart is like the proverbial apples and oranges problem. You can't deal with them together, as a single category. So, what's the point? First, quit trying to think with your heart. Thoughts, choices, decisions take place in the head. Second, make the best choices possible based on the weighing of all the issues and the evidence possible. Then live with your decision.

7. The Problem with Anger Management

Here is another language problem. The term "anger management" has become an accepted theory and part of everyday vocabulary. It appears to be something that can actually be accomplished, i.e. that anger can be managed. Many anger management counselors begin by affirming that it is all right to be angry, that anger is normal, natural and healthy. I wonder about this because I have known many individuals who became angry and did something they got into serious trouble over. I suppose it could be said that they just didn't manage their anger very well. But I doubt that anger is ever natural, normal and healthy.

Let's distinguish two types of anger. I will refer to these types as M.A.D. and R.I.D. M.A.D. (misplaced aggression decision) is unreasoned, reckless, potentially harmful, negative, and out of control. The event, the evaluation and the emotion are not logically related, not on the same level. This is anger that seeks revenge and hurtfulness. It seeks an unethical, unwarranted end. That is, there is no justification of means and end. There is no love motive. M.A.D. would be like kicking the television set because the picture is blurry; there is no rational connection between the event (blurred T.V. picture), the evaluation of the situation, and the choice of emotion. I suppose this is the type of anger you are supposed to "manage."

R.I.D. refers to what has been called "righteous indignation" (righteous indignation decision). The idea of righteousness (e.g. as discussed and proclaimed by the Old Testament prophets) seeks justice rather than revenge as a resolution to conflict. It is honorable, moral, and looks for reasonable, equitable solutions to problems. There is a justification of means and ends, and it has love as its motive. This type of anger may be practical at times. For example, you recognize an injustice against yourself or someone else and you decide something must be done about it. So, you decide upon a certain course of action: possibly litigation, or bringing pressure to bear upon the offending party. But you aren't M.A.D. in the sense of misplaced aggression decision. You are not out of control. R.I.D. is the recognition of injustice and the willingness to take appropriate action to remedy it.

Another term needs to be included here: firmness. Firmness might be thought of as a sub-heading of R.I.D. You can be firm without being M.A.D. If you are in a supervisory position you want to be firm (business like) with your employees, but you don't want to be mean to them. You can be firm without being angry. Parents must often be firm with their children for their own welfare and safety. But they can, and certainly should, do this without actually being mad (M.A.D.).

Let's restate the problem. First, the objective should not be to try to "manage" anger because anger is an emotion, and emotions cannot be managed/controlled without first managing/controlling the thought process which produced the anger in the first place. If you are M.A.D. some faulty thinking preceded it.

Second, is it really all right to be angry? Is it really normal, natural and healthy? What is the evidence for this? It is a fairly well established fact that angry (M.A.D.) people often do stupid, irresponsible, violent, illegal acts. M.A.D. type of anger is never justified. In Paul's letter to the Ephesians (New Testament, Ephesians 4:26) he says, "Be angry but do not sin; do not let the sun go down on your anger." In the Old Testament book of Ecclesiastes (7:9) is found this advice: "Be not quick to anger; for anger lodges in the bosom of fools."

Third, you do not store or stuff or repress anger and then, sooner or later, explode any more than you store joy or happiness and at some point explode. "Expressing" your anger (i.e. talking about it, "venting" it) is not the most effective method of dealing with it. In fact, it can nurture it and extend it. Getting anger "off your chest" may actually worsen the situation because listening to your own irrational arguments/excuses/victim statements can enhance your previously held views. Talking can indeed be good. But it's the quality of the talk that matters.

Fourth, ask yourself some questions: What type of anger are you experiencing? M.A.D. or R.I.D.? It is important to understand the difference. Identify your anger quickly. What is the motive behind it? Revenge, get even, save face; or righteousness, justice? Where are you going with it? What will the consequences/results be in the end? Is there a justification between means and ends? Get anger in proper perspective. Perspective has a vanishing point.

8. The Focus

The question in a nutshell is: Where should you focus? If you are trying to find a way or method to help solve your personal problems should you focus on a) thinking, b) emotions, or c) actions (behavior)? The *Diagnostic and Statistical Manual* used by psychologists and psychiatrists focuses primarily on emotions and behavior. The DSM concentrates on "emotional disorders" and "behavioral disorders." In other words, are you going to spend the rest of your life concentrating on changing your emotions and/or changing your behavior? And how do you propose to do that? You may very well need to change your emotions and your behavior, but how?

I believe the answer is that you focus on changing thinking, not on emotions and behavior. If illogical, immature thinking is examined and changed to logical, mature thinking, emotions and action/behavior will necessarily become more appropriate. It might be interesting look at the *Diagnostic and Statistical Manual* (which lists around 374 "disorders") along side a logic book which lists around thirty-eight fallacies under six categories. Earlier I listed six fallacies of the misuse of language. Other types are usually arranged as fallacies of neglected aspect, fallacies of general irrelevancies, fallacies of counterfeit evidence, fallacies of subjective irrelevancies, and fallacies of false presumption. These rather forbidding sounding categories actually include a list of names given to fallacies in thinking. If you want to improve your ability to think rationally/logically, then learning the fallacies (all or some of them) is an excellent place to start.

Medical or physical problems should be dealt with by medical/health providers. Problems with thinking (which, after all, is where problems originate) can effectively be dealt with by philosophical counselors or simply by learning to think more logically. Problems that clearly are thinking, logical problems should not be treated as "mental" or medical problems. The DSM assigns names to emotional and behavioral "disorders." Philosophy (logic) assigns names to faulty thinking, namely the logical fallacies. There is a fundamental difference.

E. Some Summary Statements

1. Feeling good about yourself is actually thinking positive thoughts about yourself based upon a certain level of achievements or accomplishments.

2. Getting in touch with your feelings may be better stated as examining your thoughts. How else can you do it?

3. Do something good if you want to feel good. Don't wait until you feel something in order to do something. Doing precedes feeling. The best antidote for simple depression or melancholia is to get involved with someone who needs your help. Find someone in a worse situation than yours (oh, yes you can) and help that person.

4. Don’t try to modify your behavior without modifying your thinking. When you think logically, maturely, you will tend to act more maturely.

5. Quit trying to think with your heart. You can’t make decisions with your head cut off. You have choices between alternatives. Make the best decisions/choices you can make, and then get on with your life.

SECTION TWO: SOLUTIONS

Event Evaluation Training (E.E.T.) is the title I use to best describe my method of helping individuals and groups to come to terms with defining and finding solutions to their problems. Everything I discuss in one way or another involves understanding this concept.

A. Premise.

My basic premise is that the things people are often bothered about are usually not so much psychological in nature as philosophical and spiritual. Therefore, traditional methods of therapy may need to be re-evaluated in the light of their overall effectiveness and in the light of other methods and techniques.

B. Postulate. T.E.A. - Thinking > Emotion > Action

When thinking changes, emotions (feelings) and actions (behavior) change accordingly. This is the thesis, the major idea of Event Evaluation Training. When thinking changes (i.e. becomes more logical, rational, mature) emotions become more appropriate and, consequently, actions (behavior) become more appropriate. The emphasis should always be on thinking (and obviously on language) rather than on emotions and actions. The order of occurrence is always T.E.A. - thinking, emotions, actions.

C. Process: The Four "E's"

1. E1 - Event: What happens or is happening; routine things, challenges of daily living; your immediate environment.

2. E2 - Evaluation: Thinking about events (analyzing, interpreting, categorizing, deciding, choosing, sifting and sorting) according to their perceived level of importance.

3. E3 - Emotion: Choices of feelings about events (E1) based on evaluation (E2). Emotion is not a given (i.e. not "automatic"); emotional levels occur in conjunction with perceived levels of events. Emotions are not always obvious or noticeable because most events are routine, expected and easily evaluated (interpreted). Otherwise, emotions are either simply positive or negative.

4. E4 - Effect: Whatever follows all the above; actually a new event or events.

D. Key

The key to this process is that E1 does not cause or produce E3. In fact E2 causes or produces E3. In other words, and in line with other cognitive models, the assumption is that things that happen (events) do not nor cannot cause or produce emotions, whether positive or negative. It is the evaluation (interpretation) of what happens that determines emotion. It is usually at this point that change in thinking needs to happen.

E. Focus

Your focus should not be on trying to change emotions (feelings) or actions (behavior). Your focus should be on changing the way you think, and the way you think about the thinking process. You can discuss or dwell on your feelings forever but nothing will change until your thinking changes fundamentally. Likewise, you can focus on your behavior, but your behavior will not change until your thinking changes radically and fundamentally.

F. A Fuller Explanation of Event Evaluation.

1. Event: Event refers simply to whatever is occurring around you, your immediate environment at any given time. It isn't necessarily something major or unusual or spectacular. In fact, most events are routine and call for no special preparation, techniques or resources. Events are your immediate experience, the business of daily living. Of course, events can also be things that happened in the past or things anticipated. Events are whatever you are dealing with (i.e. thinking about) at any given moment. The important point to remember is that things happen constantly. Events occur non-stop and simultaneously with other events in a kaleidoscopic maze of activity which you must constantly process and interpret.

2. Evaluation: You may have little or no control over events; whatever happens, happens. But you must deal with events in one way or another. Evaluation is how you choose to deal with events. It is the mental process of interpreting (i.e. sifting, sorting, analyzing, classifying) events. The evaluation process is a series of choices/decisions you make instantly and constantly. It is what you do all the time. You just need to be aware that you do it, and that sometimes you do it well and sometimes not so well, and why. Like events, evaluation is an on-going process that never ends as long as you

live. As soon as an event occurs, regardless of what it is, you evaluate it according to your perception of it, which may be right or wrong, clear or fuzzy, logical or illogical or possibly somewhere in between. And therein lies part of the problem. Your perception can be skewed and, consequently, may produce inappropriate emotions followed by equally inappropriate actions. In any case, you make decisions about events as they occur. You immediately (in a fraction of a second) categorize events (e.g. as making sense or not making sense; as threatening or non-threatening; as familiar or strange; as routine or challenging, and so on). Based upon how you evaluate events, emotions are chosen and actions (if any) are carried out. It all works together: events, perception/ evaluation, emotion, and action.

A key word in understanding the "E" formula is "appropriate." This model does not attempt to disregard or eliminate emotions (although I have sometimes been accused of trying to do that). Emotion is extremely problematic, overemphasized, and misunderstood. Emotion is hard to understand. But emotions are a necessary aspect of our humanness. While there is an obvious Stoic influence in my approach, the Stoics didn't necessarily attempt to deny a place for emotions. They simply didn't deal with emotions one way or another. Their attitude was that if life is accepted as it is, on its own terms, then there isn't much need to talk about feelings. It really doesn't matter very much how you feel. So, the objective here is not to try to ignore the importance of emotions, but to make sure that emotions and actions are appropriate to the occasion; that thinking, emotion and action are all on the same "level." (Note: Stoicism was a popular school or type of philosophy founded in 108 B.C.E. in Athens and had profound influence on Roman Culture and, to some extent, probably influenced early Christianity.)

G. Problems Do Have Solutions

The silly song sung on the T.V. comedy show "Hee-Haw" several years ago says, "If I didn't have bad luck, I'd have no luck at all." I am certain most everyone thinks like this occasionally because from time to time we do have problems, troubles or what we might call a run of bad luck. It may come as a surprise to learn that having a problem is not facing a situation for which there is no answer, no solution. I once heard a correctional officer say to an inmate, in response to her complaint about a rather trivial matter, "Just calm down, there is no problem that cannot be solved." I don't know if the inmate got the message but I certainly did. The officer's words were simple, yet profound. Problems do, indeed, have solutions. In fact, if they didn't they wouldn't be problems.

Have you ever looked up the word "problem" in the dictionary? I had never thought about it either until I heard the officer's statement. It's an interesting word. The meaning is quite different from what you may have first thought. It means "a matter proposed for solutions; a question difficult (not impossible) of solution; perplexing; anything to be worked out" (not covered up or hidden). I noticed that the word "problematic" was listed right under the word "problem." This word means "contingent, i.e. likely to occur; possible." Then I recalled that contingency plans are back-up plans, or plans to go to if the original or main plan falls through. It's like having a little emergency parachute in case the main one fails to open. The word "problem" comes from two Greek words, "pro" (forward) plus "ballin" (to throw). So, it literally means something thrown forward.

Why am I talking about problems? Because a problem appears more like a challenge to solve rather than a burden to bear. Of course, the point needs to be made that one does not have to have a problem. Today everyone is almost expected to have a problem of some sort. Having a therapist is seen by some as a status symbol. It's like having a butler or a chauffeur. (It means you can afford one.) However, it is quite all right not to have a problem.

I still remember Jeanie. She was ten years old and living in a home for children where I worked. One hot summer afternoon I was headed to my office when I saw her sitting in a chair at the end of the hallway. She was swinging her legs and staring at the floor. "Hi Jeanie," I said, "What's happening?" "Oh, nothing," she replied. "I'm just trying to have a problem." I asked Jeanie why in the world she wanted to have a problem. It was 3:30 p.m., time for her scheduled appointment with her social worker. The social worker asked her "what is your problem today?" And, alas, Jeanie didn't have one. Well, she certainly can't talk with her social worker about her problem if she doesn't have one. So the social worker told her she could sit in the chair at the end of the hallway until she thought of something they could talk about. So there she sat.

It didn't take me long to figure out what the real problem was, and I also came up with a grand solution for it. About ten minutes later Jeanie and I, along with five or six other kids who were more than willing to share our irresponsible mood that afternoon, walked into the local Dairy Queen. Point: If you have a problem, there is a solution for it. It wouldn't be a problem if there wasn't a possible solution. If your problem is that you really don't have a problem, don't try to invent one.

H. You Think You Have Problems.

I asked myself who, of everyone I know or have known or read about, has had more problems than anyone, and how was his or her problems dealt with? I immediately thought of the Old Testament character Job. Here is probably history's best example of a person who had more than his share of problems. Job is an ancient (written around 1000-800 B.C.E.) highly dramatic folktale which deals primarily with the theme of why the righteous suffer. In Rabbi Kushner's words, "Why do bad things happen to good people?"

The Job story line goes like this: In order to prove what a good man Job was, God allowed Satan to test his faith. Satan contended that if Job was stripped of everything that was important to him he wouldn't be good. In other words, Satan thought that Job was good for something rather than good for nothing. (A basic notion of the "wisdom literature" is that the wicked suffer while the righteous prosper.) So, Job lost everything: his wealth, his health and his children. He had nothing left but himself and his wife, who proved to be incapable of giving him good advice. He barely existed, and he even reached the point where he questioned the meaning of his existence. In other words, Job had major problems in several areas. How did he deal with them?

First, Job listened to his friends but he was not swayed by their arguments. In Job's case his friends, though they tried, brought him no comfort. Actually, he referred to them as "miserable comforters." They argued long and eloquently that Job's problems were due to some wrong-doing, and that if he would just repent he would be forgiven and restored to his former place in society and before God. But even in the face of such enormous pain, blame, shame and misery, Job never once questioned his own self-righteousness.

There is a tremendously important lesson here. Listen to what others have to say, weigh all points of view, but trust yourself and have confidence in your own ability to find solutions to your problems. That's the first step in solving any problem. Any and all change is up to you and you alone.

Second, Job didn't blame God or try to implicate God in even the smallest way. "In all this (i.e. his afflictions) Job did not sin or charge God with wrong" (1:22). Nor did he blame anyone or society or any particular set of circumstances for his predicament.

Later on in the story Job became frustrated over the fact that he knew that God knew his situation but allowed it to happen for no reason that he could understand. Neither Job or his three friends, in all their deliberation, pondering and weighing of the issues, could discover a logical or theological explanation for all that had happened, other than his friends formula that brokenness and poverty is the direct result of sin. And Job was not willing to yield to that indictment.

Perhaps the most juvenile, immature approach you can take is to make God the scapegoat for the disasters and calamities that come your way. By asking why did God allow this or that to happen, God is placed in a no-win situation. That is, the unwanted situation occurred because God was negligent (careless, not taking care of business), uncaring (allowed it to happen capriciously, deliberately, has a mean streak or to teach you a lesson) or powerless (couldn't have prevented the occurrence). Either way God is held responsible. In this way of viewing the cause of problems, God is either a tyrant or a wimp. Granted, the theodicy problem (i.e. if God is good, why is there evil in the world?) is as old as recorded history, but it only goes in circles and there appears to be no adequate answer in sight.

The lesson here is that in the final analysis you are responsible, you are the determiner of your destiny regardless of the problems you may have to deal with. They are your problems and you must find the solutions to your problems and the answers to your questions. If you have help along the way, so much the better; consider yourself fortunate. One of the major themes in the writings of Ralph W. Emerson is self-reliance. However, faith and self-reliance are not mutually exclusive.

Third, if Job did not blame God or others for his problems, neither did he blame himself. In fact, he never doubted his own integrity (31:6). Job said he would sign his name to a statement of innocence, a strong stance some 3000 years ago. Job's friends took the position some take today in trying to assess and determine why we have problems in the first place, that there must be something terribly wrong with someone (with myself) for the problem to occur; and God is, therefore, punishing them (me). Does this sound familiar? I asked for it. It's all my fault. I knew this was going to happen because I did thus and so. I deserve what has happened, and on and on. Granted we are the makers of most of our misery. But to whip oneself over and over for ones problems is just as wrong as trying to blame it on God.

Most of your problems you can solve on your own, if you correctly identify the problem and use appropriate solution techniques. My high school principal said the mark of an educated person is not how much knowledge he has in his head at any given moment, but whether or not he knows how to find out what he needs to know. It's much the same with solving problems. (I believe that E.E.T. provides a set of tools that will enable you to properly identify and find adequate solutions to your problems.)

There are some problems you need to own, and others you need to disown. Determining whose problem it is may be the first step in finding a solution. It may or may not be your problem. Job finally decided that his problem was as much spiritual as it was physical, so he took his case to God. To make a long, dramatically moving and beautiful story short, Job's integrity was finally upheld, and his place in society and especially his vision of himself was restored. Through a tedious and soul-searching process he solved his problems and resumed his life, probably as a better person than before. Problems, no matter how upending, do have solutions.

SECTION THREE: CHANGE

A. Change is Time, Time is Change

Carl Jung (Swiss psychoanalyst, 1875-1961) believed that problems cannot be solved, they can only be outgrown. By outgrown I think he meant that as time passes the thinking process about particular problems (events) changes. As you move away from an event your evaluation (interpretation, remembrance) of it changes which allows you to see it in a different, perhaps more positive (but perhaps not) or at least in a more rational, realistic manner. Distance (time) can improve perspective. You don't forget a problem but you remember it in a different, maybe less destructive way as you move away from it.

In the New Testament the Gospel of Luke tells of the ten lepers encounter with Jesus. When he saw the lepers he told them to go show themselves to the priest. Luke says, "And as they went (on their way) they were cleansed/healed" (17:14). It isn't the idea of a miracle that I want you to see in this story. It's the idea that as you move on things begin to change. Jung talks about the process of individuation (i.e. the pattern of unique human growth). Individuals undergo a developmental journey involving myth, archetypes, and symbols among other guideposts through life. As you move, you change, you outgrow problems by restructuring events and creating new ones: new myths, archetypes and symbols which act as new guideposts. Renewal and restoration occur as you move on because moving on involves change in thinking. (Note: Myths are stories that serve as anchors and guideposts, not lies.)

B. Do People Ever Really Change?

Since philosophers, theologians and other serious thinkers first began to ask questions about the ultimate nature of the world and reality a lot of time, energy and ink has been given to the problem of human nature. Who are we human beings? What makes us who and what we are? Are we much different, if anything, from other animals? Can we go from mere human animal to something more god-like, from anthropos to theos? Are we created in the image of God and, if so, what exactly does that mean?

Perhaps too much has been made of trying to solve the riddle of human nature. I have never read what I believe to be a satisfactory definition, much less a definitive answer, to the question of human nature, and I doubt that I ever will. The first question probably ought to be, is there such a thing as human nature? In short, can human beings ever change qualitatively or are we stuck with "human nature being what it is?"

One of the most intriguing questions ever put to me came from a woman in a correctional institution who had been diagnosed on more than one occasion as a sociopath, an anti-social personality. She asked me if I thought the diagnosis was accurate. I told her that if my understanding of the terminology in relation to my conversations with her and my observation of her was correct, then I thought the diagnosis was accurate. She then looked at me intensely and said, "If all that everyone says about me is true, is it possible for me to ever change?" I was lost for an immediate response. She had heard me say numerous times, "change the way you think." I finally told her that I thought it was possible for her to change if she really wanted to and if she was willing to make the effort, but it would not be easy. But I wasn't satisfied with my answer because I knew she had cut to the heart of a real dilemma: do sociopaths ever change? Or can they, in fact, change? And the bigger question, how?

I must admit that after many years of working with hundreds of individuals who would easily be categorized as sociopath, anti-social personality, I have seen little that would be considered real, honest, basic, nitty-gritty change. I am skeptical about the prospects of certain individuals I have known every changing. To be honest, I doubt that the woman just mentioned will ever change. I would almost bet on it. And yet, how can I be so sure? Well, of course, I can't. I wonder if I have any business even thinking that way. Ah, there's the rub. On the one hand my years of experience working with juvenile delinquents and convicted felons leads me to believe that there are individuals who will never, under any set of circumstances, change their behavior for the better. But I cannot be certain. It's like the doctrine of predestination. God may know the ultimate outcome, but no one else does. So, the only solution is to try to get everyone "saved" whether you think they are predestined or not. It would appear that a lot of work is wasted on those who, as it may turn out, are predestined.

On the other hand, I must believe that it is possible for genuine change to occur in the life of any individual regardless of their behavioral history or their diagnostic prognosis. One of the most commonly used axioms among behavioral scientists (especially those who work in criminal justice systems) is that past behavior is the best indicator of future behavior. As a general rule I believe this is a sound, reliable theory. If I want to know what your behavior is likely to be for the next year, I can look at the past year and have a pretty good idea. If I want to look at, say, the next five years, I can look at your past five and have a fairly reliable picture. This works well up to a point. Obviously, if I try to look too far ahead or too far back the picture becomes blurred and the prognosis unrealistic. In general, however, past behavior is (fortunately or unfortunately) a reasonably good indicator of future behavior.

This is both bad news and good news. The bad news is that if you take an honest, objective look at your life for the past year and you don't like what you see, then the year ahead probably doesn't hold much to look forward to. You may become discouraged and depressed (depress yourself). If you look at the past five years (or whatever amount of time you choose to consider) and you find you've not exactly been a role model for the community, the future may appear more of a threat than a promise. For the truth is, you will more than likely continue traveling the same road you're on now unless something dramatically radical happens that changes the picture.

There's also some good news. In spite of the fact that people tend to continue doing what they've been doing; in spite of the truth of the adage that past behavior is the best indicator of future behavior, people can and do change. Every religion in the world is based upon the supposition that people can change. Thinking can change and behavior can change. Every type of therapy modality I am aware of was developed ultimately as a vehicle for helping people change and improve their lives.

Sometimes change is only temporary; it lasts for a while and reverts. But sometimes change is genuine and permanent. Change often appears in the form of a slow start and a slide back, followed by another attempt until it eventually becomes more regular, habitual, and then permanent. But however it happens, it does happen. Real life-defining change is possible for anyone at anytime. This is the heart of the gospel of Jesus. This is what repentance means: to have a change of mind, to reverse direction. The basic meaning of the Greek noun "metanoia" (English "repent") is change of mind. It means to reverse direction in the sense that a company of marching soldiers does an about-face. And this is the goal of good therapy: to enable individuals to make the changes in thinking (which, consequently, effects emotions and behavior) that improves the quality of their humanness and their capacity as social beings. Yes, Virginia, people can actually and fundamentally change.

All change is precipitated by a catalyst. Something outside a particular process gets inside the process and creates or necessitates change. A catalyst is a change agent. This is the particular work of Event Evaluation Training and of cognitive therapies in general. There must be a track to run on in order for the train to move. In order for thinking to become more logical and mature there must be a way for it to happen; there must be a precipitator; in other words, a catalyst. If diligently applied E.E.T. can be that catalyst for change.

C. You Can Change the Way You Think

That you think is neither the question nor the issue. You think all the time. The problem is the way you think. You've probably said, "Oh, I just didn't think or I wouldn't have done this or that." By now it should be clear that there's something wrong with this statement. You have to think or you couldn't have done whatever you did. Actually, if you could do things without thinking, you wouldn't have much need for a brain, would you? I saw a plaque on an office wall with the single word, "think." Granted, it's probably better than other plaques I've seen, but it misses the essential point. Thinking is not an option. Thinking isn't something that can be turned on and off. But logical thinking is not always evident based upon the choice of emotions and actions that follow. You think, but you may not always think well, and you may not think much about the thinking process. So, the question isn't whether you think, but how well do you think, and, even beyond that, how well do you want to think? It is the quality of thinking that is important.

If real, authentic change in thinking is possible, how does it occur? You can change the way you think, but it isn't easy.

In fact, it's extremely difficult. There are at least four steps to consider if you expect to change the way you think. First, and foremost, you must recognize that you need to change your thinking. If you are quite happy with the way things are in your life then you have nothing to worry about; you probably don't need to change. But if there's room for some improvement (i.e. your emotions and your actions are out of proportion to events that occur, and your behavior has become unacceptable to others and to yourself), then you may want to seriously consider finding a way to change your thinking patterns. And the first step is recognition of the problem.

Second, you must make a firm decision to change. Counseling (by whatever name) cannot help unless and until you are ready and willing to change. Decision is the main ingredient of success in any endeavor. For example: There is a television advertisement that says if you want to quit smoking you will need help to do it. Actually, nothing could be further from the truth. The advertisers and marketers want you to believe that you can't stop smoking unless you purchase their product. However, the only way you will ever quit smoking (or anything else you want to quit) is to decide to quit. Smoking is a choice, a deliberate decision. If you try to stop smoking, you probably never will stop because trying is an on-going, continual process. Patches, pills and tapering off gimmicks usually do not work. Studies have shown that most people who undergo hypnosis to stop smoking begin again usually within a year or less. The failure rate is high because the smoker is depending on the proposed remedy (patches, pills, hypnosis) to solve the problem without any serious commitment to quitting. The smoker depends on the gimmick, but it doesn't work like that. I have never had anyone who has tried these so-called remedies tell me that they actually helped. The only way to stop smoking is to decide to not smoke any more. The decision is the remedy. And, yes, it's hard to do.

Third, you must commit yourself to your decision. The Lord's Prayer includes the statement, "Give us this day our daily bread." Resolve is a daily reaffirmation of a decision. Without commitment you are likely to revert back to your old thinking patterns and habits. In fact, I can almost guarantee it. Without resolve (or will-power) a decision will lack the force of action. You may start off with good intentions but you will "backslide."

Fourth, you need to periodically (possibly monthly) review and evaluate what is happening. Are you making improvements in your thinking-emotion-action? Is your thinking becoming more logical and mature, and are your emotions and actions more appropriate to the events that are occurring around you? Do those closest to you notice a change in your demeanor? And perhaps more importantly are you yourself aware of your progress? Are you following the E.E.T./T.E.A. model?

The Event Evaluation process requires daily attention. This point should be emphasized. Other types or modes of therapy may be easier and even more enjoyable. It's usually much easier to sit in a circle and swap stories, talk about how you feel, hug your neighbor and get some soft assurance that everything will be all right; that you're in a "I'm O.K., you're O.K." kind of world. And you might leave with an immediate feeling of euphoria, as though you have been "emotionally massaged". But you may quickly realize that nothing really, significant or substantial has changed. You think the same illogical, immature way; you create the same inappropriate emotions; and you behave in the same inappropriate, self-destructive, ways that may also hurt others. Each piece of the process must be in place before positive change can occur; recognition, decision, resolve, and review.

D. Insight Is Instant, Change Isn't

In comic books an idea or insight is shown as a light bulb. A "light" goes off in the mind. You have an "ah, ha" experience. But it is important to realize that a learning curve is not a straight line from zero to one-hundred (i.e. from the lower left corner of a square to the top right). A more realistic learning curve looks more like uneven stair steps. For example, you may read and study a particular subject for a certain amount of time without believing you are making much progress. But after a while it all comes together; the light goes off, and you suddenly understand, you get it. And it happens instantly. A pot of water on a hot stove will take a while to reach the boiling point, but when it reaches that point it boils instantly. The learning process will take whatever amount of time necessary. But at some particular moment you know that you know. In this sense insight is instant.

Change usually isn't instant. Change on any level, at any point, regarding virtually anything is both qualitatively and quantitatively exceedingly difficult. It is a well worn axiom that habits are hard to break. Just because you know you ought to do something (or not do something) is no guarantee that you'll do it or stop doing it. And it may be especially true that long held ideas and beliefs are hard to change, even with the evidence of new and more reliable ones. Change involves thinking; and thinking, of course, involves change.

Whatever you have done and are doing you will probably continue doing. And whatever you have believed from as far back as you can remember has a certain sacrosanct quality about it. What is important to you and what you have been taught since childhood tends to stick tenaciously with you. And that's not altogether bad. In fact, you need a certain amount of certitude, familiarity and routine in your life. You would become quite uncivilized if you had to constantly assess and reassess every situation. You need some sameness for the sake of saneness.

On the other hand, the central thesis of this book is about the willingness to change; about the need to change, in order to affect certain objectives, regarding the quality of your life. Old patterns of thinking and behavior are comfortable and routine. Change may be quite the opposite: terribly upsetting and painfully uncomfortable. Change can be like moving from a world of comfort and familiarity to a new, uncomfortable and unfamiliar one. And for some it may be easier to live with familiar demons, dragons and deserts than to figure out a way to get rid of and/or replace them. So, whatever you're currently doing, you'll tend to continue doing unless you're willing to face the challenge of making some radical (i.e. root, basic) changes in your thinking. The sober truth is: You may never change because you may not have the desire and determination to make it happen. If that's the case then no therapy program will ever work for you. It isn't the therapy model; it isn't the therapist; it isn't the "prescription" (although all these things are very important). It's you. It's the existential predicament that keeps cropping up time and time again. The old spiritual says, "It's me, it's me, it's me, O Lord, standing in the need of prayer. Not my brother, not my sister, but it's me, O Lord, standing in the need prayer." You cannot change events. You are not likely to change other people. The only variable is you. Insight is instant, but change is h-a-r-d. But remember, change is also possible.

E. How Change Occurs

Once I attended a seminar led by a psychologist who worked for the federal Bureau of Prisons on how to effectively encourage individuals (inmates in this case) to change their behavior. I thought it was an excellent seminar and I left with some good ideas. But oddly enough the thing I remember most from that seminar is that, according to the presenter, there are two primary reasons why people change their behavior: they either see the light or they feel the heat. I was amazed that I had never heard this little gem before. It may appear simplistic but I've never found any grounds on which to disagree with it. Generally I dislike either/or and black/white type statements regarding anything because most everything usually falls somewhere in the middle and is a shade of gray. However, in terms of the manner in which people actually change, the light and heat analogy is probably accurate because it involves change in thinking.

Hopefully, and maybe idealistically, people change because they see the light. They recognize that change is necessary and that the overall effect will be good. And sometimes it actually happens like that. However, I am a little more pessimistic than to think that it is the rule rather than the exception. More likely the truth is that most people change because they feel the heat. As a rule people dislike change. It's all too easy to put something off until the very last minute, until it simply has to be done, until the realization that the consequences of no change will be more severe than change. Even as I am writing, the income tax deadline is 12:00 p.m. According to post office personnel droves of people will drive to the drop-off point at the last hour, even the last minute. They know it has to be done but they wait until they feel the heat.

My point is this: In order for the Event Evaluation Training method to be most effective you need to see the light. You must be able to calculate the difference between where you are and where you want to be, and have the willingness (resolve) to get there. It is a deliberate process. If you try to change the way you think by waiting until you feel the heat (e.g. as you approach each event/situation) you may never reach your goal of becoming a more rational and mature person. You will always be trying to catch up after the fact. (The "oh-I-could-have-had-a-V.8" kind of thinking.) If you feel the heat you have probably waited too long and you end up viewing the T-E-A process in some other order. In other words, if your action (behavior) is based upon feeling the heat (e.g. pressure from others, threat, embarrassment, saving face) your evaluation of the event may not be accurate, which means, of course, that your emotion and action will probably not be appropriate. And if this is the case, then you are likely to repeat the process over and over because positive change in the thinking process has not occurred (i.e. you have not yet seen the light). You are merely doing what you think you must at the moment in order to get by the immediate difficult situation. Individuals whose actions occur because they feel the heat never get beyond a stay-ahead-of-the-posse mentality. Unfortunately these are individuals who are repeat offenders, who are in and out of prison, and who engage in the same irrational, destructive, self-defeating behavior while thinking that things will be different or better the next time. When the only logical move is to get away from the heat, seeing the light becomes the only viable solution.

The story is told of a young Japanese man who wanted to become enlightened but he apparently did not know how to go about it. After seeking the advice of some knowledgeable individuals he decided to travel to a remote island and study with a Zen master for a period of three years. At the end of the three years the young man had not experienced enlightenment. He expressed his frustration to the master and informed him of his intention to return home. The master said, "You've been here three years; stay three months more." The young man agreed. But at the end of this period he still had not become enlightened and he informed the master again that he was leaving the island. The master said, "You've been here three years and three months; stay three weeks more." The student stayed but he was no closer to becoming enlightened than before. The master, sensing his intense disappointment, said, "You've been here three years, three months, and three weeks. Stay three days more. However, if at the end of that time you still have not attained enlightenment you must commit suicide." Towards the end of the third day the student was enlightened.

The amazing thing is that no one can tell you how to become "enlightened" (seeing the light instead of constantly feeling the heat; figuring out what is good for you and what isn't; what works and what doesn't).There's nothing magic about it. You simply have to weigh the issues and make decisions you can (indeed must) live with. Understanding both your tremendous freedom and responsibility, and the permanence of choices and consequences, is certainly the first step in becoming an enlightened person. This realization helps put everything else in perspective. And, it shouldn't take three years, three months, three weeks, and 3.9 days to reach this point. Learning/knowledge is gradual; insight/enlightenment is instant.

F. Mental Imaging - If You Think It, You Can (Probably) Do It.

One winter evening while watching the Olympics skiing events on T.V. I became interested in one particular skier who, while waiting his turn, appeared to be praying. His head was slightly bowed and his eyes were closed. I imagined that he was saying something like, "O, God, help me to ski well. Help me to not fall down and kill myself, or at least to not embarrass myself in front of millions of people. Give me a safe trip down the mountain." Something like that. But just then the announcer said that he was focusing on his run. He was actually imagining making the run down the long slope successfully. He was "seeing" himself skiing at his top speed, rounding the turns, making the jumps and crossing the finish line in fine form. In other words, the skier imagined being successful. Of course, focusing in this way isn't too different from prayer. Prayer is a way of getting ones thoughts in order and focusing on what's important, on what needs to be done, and how to do it. Mental imaging is a form of prayer and vice versa. But whatever you want to call it, it's highly effective.

When I was in high school, our thespian troupe was about to present a play. Minutes before the curtain was to go up Martha was walking back and forth saying "I just know I'm going to forget my lines; I just know it. I'm going out there and make a fool of myself; I just know it." Well, guess what? With a kind of Charlie Brown pessimistic prediction she forgot her lines and made a fool of herself. Why? Because she said she was going to. She imagined herself failing. Of course, she may have messed up regardless. But she would have been on much safer ground if she had imagined herself going on stage and "bowling them over."

You tend to do what you imagine yourself doing. If you're in a difficult or stressful situation you can mental image up or down. You can think your way to failure or to success. Granted you may not fail just because you imagine yourself failing, and you may not succeed just because you imagine yourself succeeding. But the chances of handling a difficult situation well will be greatly increased if you think through a scenario that leads step by step to a successful conclusion.

Suppose you are having problems with a particular individual. Imagine a conversation with this person in a specific setting. Imagine what he says, what you say, back and forth; but imagine yourself handling the situation in a logical, mature manner. Imagine a successful ending. Maybe not a "perfect" ending, but an ending you can live with. That, in essence, is what mental imaging is all about. In a sense you do this all the time because you think (evaluate) all the time. The idea is to do it deliberately and in a certain direction. You will be much more likely to make it down the slope without falling, and to remember your lines.

G. How Do You See Yourself?

Sociologists insist, quite correctly I believe, that the way you view yourself is largely socially determined. That is, you learn everything, including the way you think about yourself, from others. It is very important what others think about you. But your view about that is based upon what you think others think about you.

Sociologist Charles Horton Cooley is famous for his "Looking Glass Self," a theory of how individuals arrive at their sense of self. Cooley said: "Each to each a looking glass, reflects the other that doth pass." The Looking Glass Self has three components which may be summarized in the following manner:

1. I'm not who I think I am.
2. I'm not who you think I am.
3. I am who I think you think I am.

According to the *Concise Oxford Dictionary of Sociology* (Gordon Marshall, Ed., 1994) the first part is the imagination of your appearance to others; the second part is the imagination of their judgment of that appearance; and the third part is your feelings such as pride, shame, and so on. In other words, the entire process is based upon your evaluation (assessment/interpretation) of the way you think others think about you.

"I'm not who I think I am" implies that you can be wrong about yourself. You can over or under rate/value yourself. You may have abilities that you don't see but others do. Or the opposite might be true. You might not always be able to trust your own thoughts and feelings about yourself because you might not be seeing the entire picture of yourself.

"I'm not who you think I am" implies that, just as you can be wrong about yourself, others can be wrong about you also. Even your best friend has limited knowledge of the "real" you. There may be things that even your spouse isn't aware of about you (e.g. your deepest longings and desires, your highest or "secret" ambitions, your spiritual nature, and so on).

"I am who I think you think I am" is the truer picture. You see yourself as you perceive the way others see you. Another way to state this is, you tend to act in ways you think others expect you to act. This is the mirror effect of Cooley's theory. You take your cue from the way you think (right or wrong) others expect you to behave. This is why children who are constantly told they are bad, no good and will never amount to anything may tend to act out what they think is expected of them. If you are constantly told you are stupid, you will tend to see yourself as a stupid person. Of course, the Looking Glass theory holds true for adults as well as for children.

Another way to answer the question of how you see yourself is suggested by Johann Wolfgang Von Goethe (18th-19th Century German writer/poet): "If you treat people as they are, they will always remain as they are. But if you treat them as you wish them to become, they will tend to become that better person." This idea can be applied in a variety of ways and settings (e.g. parent-child relationships; employer-employee relations). Cooley and Goethe are making similar points only in different ways. Namely, that your self-image is strongly influenced by the image you think others have of you. It's a two-sided coin. If you are influenced by what you think others think of you, others are likewise influenced by what they think you think of them. Goethe's idea is probably one side of the coin and Cooley's the other. Cooley emphasizes understanding the way you see yourself, and Goethe emphasizes that you have the capacity to be a positive influence on others. Your idea of yourself (and ultimately your behavior) is largely a reflection of the way you think others see you.

Robert Burns, in *To A Louse,* sums up self-perception poetically:

O wad some power the gifte gie us

To see ourselves as ithers see us!

It wad frae monie a blunder free us,

And foolish notion:

What airs in dress an' gait wad lea's us,

And ev'n devotion.

Burns was recollecting a childhood scene in church one Sunday when a louse was crawling up the ribbon of the bonnet of a well-dressed, sophisticated lady who was unaware of its presence. How silly she must have looked to a young boy, and how out of place she (and the louse) must have appeared. If the lady could have seen herself as Burns saw her, she might not have thought of herself as looking so sophisticated. The truth is, while Cooley and Goethe are correct in their notion about how self-image is formed, Burns is also quite perceptive in that you don't always see yourself as others see you. All three would probably agree that it's the way you think you see that is the determining factor.

Having this knowledge should inform your thinking-emotion-action process. If you know that you tend to act as you think others expect you to act, then you should be able to avoid the trap of thinking you must always act in certain prescribed, habitual ways. Self-image will, at least to a certain extent, always reflect the way you think others see you. In fact, it is a useful and necessary gauge of your social environment and well-being. But you must also learn to see yourself beside the mirror (which is probably harder to do). Look in the mirror to see yourself, and look also in yourself to see yourself and others.

H. Change and Control

When following the Event Evaluation Training model it should become clear that you cannot change events. You cannot change others. One of the fundamental notions of any cognitive therapy program is that things cannot be different than they are. If another person's behavior is bad, out of control or otherwise inappropriate and unacceptable you will probably be wasting your time trying to change that person's thinking or behavior. In any event (situation) the only variable is you. Wishing that things could or should have been different than they are at any given moment is sheer nonsense, not to mention faulty logic. The only thing you can change is your own evaluation/assessment/interpretation of events. This point cannot be overemphasized.

There seems to be a lot of confusion about control. A lot of time is spent trying to control the behavior of others. Political dynasties have existed throughout history based on the attempt to control masses of people, which is what totalitarianism means. It works for a while but it is never ultimately successful because people resist being controlled, and they will usually find a way to break the bonds of tyranny. It is fruitless and frustrating to try to change the behavior of others, either a large group or a single individual. Coercion in any form is unwelcome and is usually seen as a form of manipulation.

Rather than focusing on trying to change the thinking and behavior of others, switch the focus to yourself. Self-control has always been a major objective of successful individuals. One of the central tenants of Stoicism is the ability to remain in control regardless of the circumstances. One famous stoic, the Roman Emperor and philosopher Marcus Aurelius, was known for his emphasis and insistence on self-control. A major theme of the wisdom literature of the Old Testament (especially the Proverbs) is self-control.

It is impossible to control others, at least with any degree of success. In the first place why would you even want to try to control someone else's behavior? It certainly won't make you or the other person any happier. Trying to control people or things that you really have no business controlling will only lead to a less than happy outcome. When you think about it you will probably recall that the times in your life that have been the worst, the most embarrassing, the least happy, the most frustrating and the least productive have been those times when you were least in control of yourself (i.e. your thoughts, emotions and actions). Self-control begins with thought control.

I. Two (Almost) Miracle Questions

When conflicts arise there are two questions you can ask yourself that can help clarify the issues and clear the air immediately. First, is it really a problem? Just because something was a problem in the past doesn't mean it is now, at this particular time. And, what's more, you may have a better sense of how to define a problem now than you did at some time in the past. You may now think more logically and maturely than you used to. Asking if something really is a problem can help you get a second opinion (your own). And it can help you determine whether it is a situation that is really worth your time and energy to deal with. By simply asking the question you may decide it is merely an apparent conflict, not something you need to concern yourself about. If the event is not really a problem then, obviously, you shouldn't define it as a problem. If you define the event as a problem then, of course, you will need to determine a logical course of action. But in any case, you still need to ask the question.

The second question is whose problem is it? You may have already determined that there is no problem, in which case that is the end of the matter. But if you still haven't decided, or if you think the situation might actually be a problem, try to determine who has the problem. Is it your problem or someone else's? For example: If two individuals are arguing over something that is clearly none of your business, then you would be wise to consider the matter their problem and not yours. That should be simple enough. Now, suppose an individual with whom you are talking becomes irate, for whatever reason, and produces the middle finger for you to see (I think the proper term is "shooting a bird," or "up yours." I've heard many definitions). Ask yourself, do I have a problem here? Granted, you probably would rather not be confronted with such ridiculous, immature behavior. But who really has the problem? It isn't your problem that this person is acting in such a manner. It is his problem. He is the one demonstrating a lack of self-control and an inability to deal effectively with his own frustrations. You may feel sorry for him and want to help him. But his actions are not your problem.

Another point to remember is that the irate individual gesturing with his middle finger (and probably making some pretty nasty remarks) can do that if he wants to. You may not like it or want to put up with it, but it's his choice and his right to make a fool of himself if he wants to. Why should you create a problem for yourself simply because this guy is having a problem? There is no logical connection. The point is, if someone else is having a problem it is his or her problem alone. It isn't your problem, so leave it alone.

J. How Right Thinking Heals

Example One: A newspaper article (by Shankar Vedantam of the Washington Post, printed in the Louisville Courier-Journal, May 7, 2002) entitled *Depression Studies Find Placebo Effect*) states that "after thousands of studies, hundreds of millions of prescriptions and tens of billions of dollars in sales, two things are certain about pills that treat depression: antidepressants like Prozac, Paxil and Zoloft work. And so do sugar pills." The article also states that "the medicine's greatest benefits may come from the care and concern shown to patients during a clinical trial."

Example Two: A well known experiment at the Western Electric Company in Chicago (1924-1936) produced what became known as the "Hawthorne Effect." Briefly, any changes made by management in an attempt to improve the working conditions of employees at the company resulted in increased production. The researchers concluded that the variations in output were not caused by changing physical conditions or by material rewards but partly by the experiments themselves. That is, the workers responded positively to the fact that management took an interest in them.

Example Three: A popular adage often printed in church bulletins is "prayer changes things." Somewhere I read a variation on that theme by Lon Ray Call: "Prayer doesn't change things. Prayer changes people, and people change things." In any case, it's the idea of prayer as a vehicle for change that I want to emphasize. You may have heard someone say (or you may yourself have said) I felt so much better after I prayed. And it's true. Assuming that you are a person of faith who believes that God "answers" prayer, you will most likely feel better following sincere prayer. There are at least two reasons why this is true. First, you believe God is listening, otherwise you probably wouldn't be praying. That, in itself, is pretty awesome: believing that the creator/sustainer of the universe is actually listening to your prayer. Second, if prayer is to mean anything, you are focusing on issues that are very important to you. You are getting your thoughts in order of priority. You are examining matters of central and ultimate importance. Either one or both of these reasons can have a tremendous impact.

Example Four: Another old adage advocates that "time heals all things." This, also, is true for most people in most situations. The passage of time usually brings a healing perspective and a positive change of attitude regardless of how terrible or catastrophic some events may have been.

Example Five: Your mother was right: you should count to ten before you do something you might come to regret.

Now, what do these examples all have in common? In one sense, of course, nothing. But there is a common thread, a theme that connects them. The common element is that, in each case, thinking changed. The patients who were given sugar pills believed they were being helped by someone who cared about their welfare. Therefore, their thinking became more positive and more conductive to therapy (healing). When their thinking became more logical their emotions, and consequently their behavior, became more appropriate. They experienced healing because they believed they were involved in the healing process.

The Western Electric employees appreciated the fact that management took an interest in their working environment and took actions to improve conditions. As they thought about what management was doing, their thinking about the entire matter changed. Their positive thinking created more positive emotions and actions. When their thinking changed everything else changed.

In prayer you believe God is listening and that your situation will likely improve. Again, your thinking becomes more positive. You "center down" (a term borrowed from a seminary professor) on what is really important to you. Also, as you pray your thinking gradually changes from thoughts of how bad things are or seem at the moment to the possibility that things can improve. This new, more logical thinking produces more appropriate emotions which prompts more appropriate actions.

Is it really accurate to say that time heals? In and of itself time doesn't actually "do" anything. All actions and activities operate within a certain time frame. It is true that over a period of time people tend either to come to terms with unfortunate events or, at least, learn to deal with them in a less destructive, more mature manner. But why does this happen? What factors or dynamics are operative to permit or encourage this change to occur?

I believe two things account for the change, the healing. First, and most important, change in thinking occurs. You do not view an event in exactly the same way one, five, ten or twenty years after it occurred. As you grow older (i.e. as you live your life day by day) you experience innumerable other events that have various degrees of impact on your world view. You meet people, you do things, you go places and, in short, you involve yourself in a host of activities and events. The older you become (i.e. the more that time passes) the more events your mind/memory must manage. And, in the process, your thinking is bound to change regarding many things. In effect, you change your mind and rearrange your priorities.

Second, over a period of time, perspective changes. Perhaps this is simply another way of saying the same thing (i.e. thinking changes) but with a different twist. Original events, as historical entities, do not change. But they may gradually become interpreted differently. And you come to view them in relation to and in comparison with other subsequent events. In a sense you come to give events a ranking in terms of extremely traumatic, very bad, not all that bad and so on. (Remember the "levels" discussed earlier.) What once appeared as a five on the thought-emotion-action Richter scale may later get re-ranked as a three or two. Perspective does not have to change over time, but it often does. At least enough time must expire in order for a comparison between old and new views of events to become evident.

Imagine that you and a friend are standing beside a long, straight road. You each say good-by and your friend begins walking down the road while you stand and watch. For a few seconds she looks about the same as when you stood right beside her. But after a minute she looks smaller. After five minutes she looks much smaller. And after a while longer she will appear to disappear over the horizon. You believe she is the same person even though, in appearance, she gradually became smaller and finally left your field of vision. If five years go by will you continue to think about your friend in exactly the same way as the day she left you standing in the road? Probably not. Much water will have flowed under the bridge, so to speak. Your thinking will have changed to one degree or another. Time (thinking) produces changes in memory, perception and views of the relative importance of events. You may miss her after five years but the intensity may be different.

If you count to ten before taking an action what, essentially, are you doing? You are allowing time to pass, and the passing of time permits (actually necessitates) change in thinking. In terms of the thinking process, ten seconds is a long time for the simple reason that there can be a profound shift in thinking in just a few seconds. Counting to ten is not what makes the difference; waiting and thinking is. Generally the longer you wait the better decisions you will make. This is why you should wait a few seconds before starting to answer a question (for, example, during an interview). The more you ponder the more likely you will give a better response.

I call this the "ping pong" effect. I learned from playing opponents who were much better than me that if you wait as long as you can (even for half a second) to return the ball you will be more likely to have a good return. If you get in a hurry you are more likely to have a bad return. You can actually do a lot of thinking (planning, preparing) in a second. Waiting is thinking. And good thinking is more likely to produce good results.

In all the above examples different dynamics were at work, and certainly more than one single conclusion can be drawn. However, without appearing overly simplistic, thinking is what made the difference. The thinking process, and the resulting change in thinking, was the common element in all the examples. And in each case it was the positive, logical thinking process that made the difference. Right thinking heals.

K. How the Prodigal Son Got Back Home

One of the most amazing and enduring stories in all literature is Jesus' parable of the Prodigal Son. Jesus didn't use the term prodigal, but it is an apt description and it has stuck to basically describe the young man's situation. A summary of the story might go like this: When Junior reached his eighteenth birthday he decided to try a short-cut approach to success, and he came up with a plan that would put him way ahead of the pack. He asked his father to give him his share of the inheritance now instead of waiting until his father grew old or died and everyone had to wait for a will to be processed. This wasn't a bad idea considering that Junior could use the money early in life when perhaps he needed it most. Surprisingly the father agreed, and after a trip to the bank and the tying together of some necessary threads, the young man was on his way to fame and fortune. At least, that's what was supposed to have happened. A lot is crammed into verse thirteen (Luke 15:13): "Not many days later the younger son gathered all he had and took his journey into a far country, and there he squandered his property in loose living." (If the stock marked dropped that fast it too would crash.)

To one extent or another, the story of the Prodigal Son is the story of every man and woman who has ever lived. It is truly a parable about the life of "Everyman," to mention John Bunyan's famous character. Who of us has not started out upon some journey or venture only to have it go sour. And we found ourselves in a situation so strange, different and humiliating that we might as well have been in a foreign country. We found ourselves destitute, physically, spiritually and maybe financially, and at our wits end wondering how in the world we could have gotten so far off track; wondering how we could have wandered so far from home, and not knowing for sure how to get back.

Sam Keen wrote a book entitled *Beginnings Without End,* (Harper and Row, 1975) in which he candidly tells how he left his family and his academic career in search of what he thought was something exciting and wonderful, only to eventually find himself lost in a wilderness, a foreign land, feeling alone and depressed. It was a place of his own creation but it didn't represent his best creativity. Sam Keen's story is about how he finally found a home, an oasis, in the midst of the wilderness. He decided not to try to go back home.

But what about those who are afraid of the wilderness, who can't find an oasis and who discover that the foreign country is more overwhelming than they had imagined? Can they ever find their way back home? The story of the Prodigal Son is a reminder that no one has to live in the wilderness if they don't want to; that there is a way back from spiritual exile, from the humiliation of living in abject spiritual poverty in a strange place. The Prodigal's exile, like that of most people, was self imposed. He went to the "far country" of his own choosing, and only his desire to change his situation would get him on the right road again. Let's look more closely at the Prodigal. What are the conditions of his returning home? What had to happen in order for him to reverse the process that had taken him so far off course?

“He came to himself (verse 17).” There are a variety of ways to approach this idea. It is rich with possibilities. This young man had to face the facts. He was a long way from home, broke, hungry, without a single friend, extremely humiliated from having to stoop to working on a pig farm in order to survive, and immensely unhappy. Things had not worked out at all the way he had anticipated when he left home.

Before he could change his situation he had to realize and accept defeat. He had to surrender to the notion that he had made a bad decision; actually a series of bad decisions. Now, a very important fact emerges at this point. He had come to be “beside himself.” His life was out of sync, out of kilter. He was not well/whole. His life was so bent out of shape, his thinking so warped, that he no longer recognized himself. He had lost sight of who he was. When he looked into the mirror he saw a stranger, not his father’s son. He used to be wealthy, now he was poor. He once was happy, now he was miserable. He once had a good home and family who cared for him. Now he was in a strange place where no one cared what happened to him. He didn’t belong to anyone or anything. He had no place and no purpose. He came to see himself as someone else, someone other than who he really was, and it was a frightening experience. He experienced a kind of spiritual amnesia. You can almost hear his father say as he went out the door, “Now son, take care of yourself and don’t forget who you are.” But he didn’t, and he did.

If you have ever been so depressed, so lost, so lonely that you came to see yourself as a different person, a stranger to yourself, then you might be able to understand what this young man was going through. I think people who commit suicide must come to this point where life becomes so painful that they see themselves as someone or something other than who they are. And they want to get rid of that “other” person. They literally loose their sanity (i.e. their humanity). They lose their sense of wholeness and, instead, come to see life in bits and pieces. People like this may be said to be "beside themselves." Or they may be what psychologists refer to as having split personality or schizophrenia.

Fortunately the Prodigal Son "came to himself" before he reached a point of no return. Some are not so fortunate. Many such individuals hurt themselves and/or others. They commit acts of violence or they deteriorate spiritually and their lives become wrecked and ruined beyond recognition. But, he came to himself. This is the difference. He figured out what he needed to do to correct it. He "got it together." He resolved his dilemma.

Notice his plan. In brief outline form here are the steps he took in order to rescue himself:

1) "He came to himself." This shows tremendous insight and maturity. For the first time in a quite a while, he began to think logically again. That was the turning point.

2) He said, "I…" He had to decide for himself. No one was there to help him. Verse sixteen says "no one gave him anything." He had no therapist or social worker or friend.

3) "Will…" The power of decision is both liberating and necessary. He didn't say ought, might, probably will, but "will." Resolve is the factor most often omitted and the reason many good intentions fall apart.

4) "Arise…" The Greek meaning is that he literally got up from a sitting or lying position. This had to occur before the first step toward home could be taken. He reinstated his own integrity. "Arise" may also recognize the spiritual aspect of the situation.

5) "…and go." Go where? Away from this miserable place, this "far country;" back home, back to his father. Where else could he go except to where he got off track in the first place?

6) “And he arose and came to his father.” In a flash of brilliant insight he knew what he had to do, he formulated a simple but sound plan, and he stuck with it.

The story has a happy ending because the father, without any questions or conditions, forgave his son and restored him to his former place in the family. All the steps the prodigal took were necessary. He couldn’t have returned home if he had tried to skip one step or take a short-cut. That’s where he went wrong at the outset. The story (not including the part about the older brother) ends with the father saying, “This my son was dead, and is alive again; he was lost, and is found. And they begin to make merry.”

SECTION FOUR: APPLICATIONS

A. What Is It About Love You Don't Understand?

Love is one of the most misused and misunderstood concepts in the English language. Some languages have more than one word for love which helps clarify the intended meaning. In English love has virtually as many meanings and variations as you wish. You can say you love your spouse, your children, your car, your pet, and certain kinds of food and music. You fall in love, out of love and manage to make love somewhere in between. But regardless of the context in which it is used love is almost always used as an expression of how you feel about someone or some-thing.

While English is a rich, beautiful and practically universal language, a single word often must be used (and, therefore, interpreted) in a variety of ways. Without understanding the context the word love would be difficult to define. In contrast the Greek has three words for love (two of which are used in the koine of the New Testament): agape, phileo and eros. Agape might be called a strong expression and phileo a weak expression (although that isn't a totally accurate description). Agape is the word used in the familiar John 3:16 (for God so loved the world), and phileo is used by Paul (Romans 12:10) to mean brotherly affection. Eros was avoided by the New Testament writers probably because it had acquired a vulgar connotation. It is from eros that the English word erotic is derived. (The meaning of eros probably lies somewhere between Plato and Hugh Hefner.)

The point I want to make is that a correct understanding of love is at the core of the ethical enterprise and, therefore, basic to understanding how to effect fundamental changes in the thinking process. Love is not based on feeling, but on doing. In fact, love has virtually nothing to do with emotion. Love has everything to do with action. Love is not about how you feel, but about what you do.

Jesus said, "Love your enemy." If love is having a feeling about someone, then Jesus' injunction would make no sense; it would be quite impossible. Two thousand years ago people thought Jesus was crazy, even dangerous, for saying those words because they (like perhaps the majority of people today) thought of love as feeling. But love isn't feeling, it's doing. Love means, first of all, acting in your own best interest, and then acting toward others in their best interest. The strongest biblical image of God is that "God is love." (1 John 4:8 "He who does not love does not know God, for God is love.") Imagine this text reading: "He who does not feel does not know God, for God is feeling." God is not love because God has warm, cozy feelings about creation, but because God is constantly at work saving, salvaging and shaping creation. God worked at creation and still works re-creating, redeeming and restoring. God is love because God acts in creation's best interest.

If you say you love someone then you must act toward that person in her best interest (which, of course, isn't always easy to determine). In this sense, love is actually a process rather than a spur-of-the-moment decision. It doesn't mean that you feel a particular way about her. If love is defined as merely how you feel at any particular moment you probably never would get beyond that feeling. What's more, you likely wouldn't feel the same in all circumstances and situations, or even from one day to the next. Love as feeling would be very inconsistent. But love doesn't mean feeling a particular way at a particular time. Love is doing what needs to be done at a particular time, using whatever resources are available. Immanuel Kant expressed the same idea: "Treat every man as an end in himself and never as a means only."

One of the best examples of how the love principle operates is Jesus' parable of the "Good Samaritan." A man (a Jew) was attacked, severely beaten, robbed and left for dead beside the road by a gang of outlaws. A priest, and later a Levite, came by and saw him but didn't bother to offer assistance. Then a Samaritan came by. (Remember that the Jews and Samaritans hated each other. That was the religious-socio-politico ideology at that time.) So, in keeping with the spirit of the times the Samaritan probably didn't like the Jew, wounded or not. And no one would have thought less of him if he, too, had ignored the wounded man. Yet, he defied the convention of the day by loving him. He didn't ask himself how he felt or was supposed to feel about the situation. He asked himself what needed to be done in order to save the Jew's life. Then he went about doing it. (Incidentally, love in the New Testament is sometimes translated as charity, or love in action, love at work.)

What the Samaritan did for the mugged Jew was love in its profoundest, clearest expression. He didn't go over to the man and tell him how sorry he was to see him in that condition. He didn't tell him he would ask his prayer group to remember him. The gospel writer (Luke 10:33-35) uses a number of verbs of action to express love: he came, saw, had compassion (or pity, i.e. he recognized the need), went, bound, poured, set, brought, took, took care of, paid, will repay. He even stayed with him through the night. In other words, the Samaritan did exactly what needed to be done in order to save the wounded Jew. How he felt never came up. It wasn't an issue. Love is about doing, and doing is ultimately what matters. Understanding and applying the principle of love is necessary to the advancement of the human enterprise. It is absolutely essential.

Love, properly understood, does not rule out the possibility for romantic relationships. Eros is natural, normal and necessary. It involves both affection and physical activity, both passion and compassion. Sexual, sensual, erotic love is an important, even necessary, part of being human. It is, in fact, how everyone gets into this world, is it not? At the same time it is important to remember that while eros is a different form/expression of love it is, nonetheless, based upon the notion of acting in the best interest of yourself and others. I mentioned earlier that the Samaritan probably didn't like the Jew (and visa versa). Like is not a synonym for love. Like is a term of affection. The Samaritan didn't like the Jew, perhaps because he didn't really know him. There was no natural affectionate bond between them. But, then, like and love are different terms and have different purposes. You don't have to like everyone. A certain individual may have characteristics, personal habits, behaviors or quirks that you find annoying, disgusting or otherwise unacceptable. You are not required to like this person. But, if you take humanity and civility seriously; if you are going to, as a matter of principle, function in the world as a decent human being (regardless of your particular religious orientation or whether you even claim to be a person of faith), then you must love other people, all people. Love is actually carrying out the "golden rule:" Do unto others (i.e. act toward others) as you would want them to do unto you (i.e. act toward you). "Do" unto others does not express the same idea as "feel" for others. Love is acting in your own best interest and then acting in the best interest of others. It begins with you. Jesus said, "Love your neighbor as yourself."

When I was a teenager there was a man in my community whom I particularly admired. He seemed to have all the qualities I wanted to have as I became an adult. He had a plaque hanging in his office which read: "God first, others second, I'm third." This was his motto and it apparently served him well for he was a very successful man. Throughout the years I have thought a lot about that motto. And I have gradually come to see it as an inverted pyramid. It doesn't balance well. In fact, it's upside down. My experience and understanding of love is the opposite. I must love myself first. That is, I must come to understand and do what is in my own best interest. Love is not selfish (1 Corinthians 13:4) so it cannot be from a self-centered motive that I love myself. It is simply where it has to begin. I must love myself (i.e. get my own life in good order) before I can effectively reach out to my family, my friends, and my community. This means understanding and being sensitive to my own needs, not in a self-centered, narcissistic way, but in a self-assessing and self-maintaining way. Until I am strong for and within myself I cannot be strong for others. If I must love my neighbor as myself, then I must love myself before I can even begin to understand how to love my neighbor.

As you begin loving yourself on a continuing basis you can begin to include others into your circle of love. Only then will you be able to adequately love others. Remember, love is not based on feeling, but on doing. If an individual is in the lake struggling to keep from drowning, she does not want shouts of encouragement (although it probably would be helpful), and she doesn't care how you may feel about her at the moment. What she really wants is for you to throw a rope, swim or row out to get her, or at least go get someone else who can help save her. Loving the person in the lake involves acting in her best interest, namely, getting her to shore. It matters little whether you like her or she likes you. You may never have even met her. But it matters immensely and profoundly that you love her.

The plaque on the wall started out with God first. So, where is God in all this talk of love? It may not be important to some, but it is extremely important for others. It may appear that God got left out or wound up at the bottom. But that's not the case at all. Jesus said, in principle, that when you love yourself and others you are, simultaneously, loving God. In fact, how else can you love God? You don't start with trying to love God, then getting around to loving Jane and John, and then reluctantly, finally pulling yourself into the picture. If you love yourself, then others, you are, at the same time, loving God. The corrected motto (in my opinion) can be stated as: Love yourself + love others = loving God.

When you change the way you think about love and apply the love principle appropriately you will have gone a long way toward improving your self-image and your relationships with others. When Jesus talked about love twenty centuries ago it was a radical, revolutionary idea. And it still is if love is understood as a verb of action. George Macdonald said, "Think of something you ought to do, and go and do it…heed not your feelings; do your work." That is the only definition of love you will ever need.

B. Relationships

It could be stated with a fair amount of accuracy that the entire human enterprise is involved with and revolves around relationships. Human beings must, to one extent or another, relate to each other. There's no way around it. There is the occasional recluse or hermit, but I doubt that they are very happy. Relationships can be good or bad but usually not avoided. It is only in community that you understand yourself and your relationship to others. Forming, building and maintain relationships is one of the most important things you do, and it is an ongoing process. Of course, sometimes it may be necessary to terminate a relationship (in the sense that any relationship actually ends), which may be simply another way of saying that decisions are made about new directions and opportunities.

James Luther Adams, a professor at the Harvard Divinity School for many years, said that human beings are always confronted with the intimate and the ultimate. You might say the here and the hereafter (although that's probably not exactly what Adams meant). But by the intimate I think he meant to recognize the importance of relationships. In one sense, it's all human beings do: meet, see, hear, communicate with, confront other human beings. Think about it:

Most of the problems you have ever had, are now having, or probably ever will have, involve other people. Most of your happiness, your successes, your sense of well being and your worst fears involve other people. Your joys and your sorrows relate to others. You cannot avoid others, and they also must contend with you. How your relation/ship sails is mostly up to you, your view of yourself and of others. If you are a crew of one, then you are definitely in a sea of trouble. If you think in terms of community, cooperation and commitment then your ship should sail more smoothly even if the waters get rough.

I have already mentioned Immanuel Kant, Charles Horton Cooley, and Johann Wolfgang von Goethe in various contexts. Each also had a lot to say, either directly or indirectly, about relationships. Jewish philosopher Martin Buber, in *I and Thou* (1922), connects several ideas by saying that if you have ever had a "bad" relationship it might be obvious to you that trust and commitment cannot be built on treating another person as an "it," as an object or means. And, by the same token, you don't want to be treated like that either.

Respect is at the core of good relationships. In my opinion this is probably the single most important factor in the school and workplace shootings that have occurred in the United States in recent years, and still occur on a regular basis. In every case that I am aware of the shooters had sensed immense disrespect on the part of fellow students and fellow employees or employers. Either rapidly, or most likely over a period of some time, this idea of not being respected, of being ignored (which, by the way, gets to the core of self-identity, self-worth, existence or non-existence) manifest itself in inappropriate (violent) behavior. Obviously the thinking process of those who commit acts of violence is irrational, and each person is responsible for his actions. However, deliberate and persistent disrespect (treating people as means, using people only to get what you want, attacking the vulnerabilities of others) will eventually not only destroy relationships but will encourage irrational thinking-emotion-actions on the part of the perpetrator of violence. The other side of the fence is to take Goethe's point of view, that you need to see beyond the immediate set of circumstances, beyond an individual's obvious shortcomings and mishaps and see her potential.

W.I. Thomas (1863-1947) stated in his well-known theorem: "When you define situations as real, they become real in their consequences." This idea is sometimes called a self-fulfilling prophesy (the word "prophesy" is used here in the popular sense of prediction, and not in the theological sense which means something quite different). An example of what Thomas is talking about is the stock market crash which occurred on October 29, 1929, due to the misguided notion (which people apparently didn't understand at that time) that everyone should get their money out of the banks because the stock market was going to crash. So, everyone got their money out of the banks (or as much as they could; actually all the money wasn't in the banks) and, consequently, the stock market crashed.

What in the world does this have to do with relationships? A lot if you consider the fact that judgments are made about other people based on bad information (gossip, skewed opinions, outright lies) about those people. Suppose an employee, George, gets transferred from one department to another, which happens to be yours. Your friend who worked with George says to you, "I'm glad he's out of our department. I really feel sorry for you guys. He's a real jerk." If you take your friend's remark seriously you've already got a problem with George and you haven't even met him. If you define George as a jerk, then (at least until you get to know George better and verify that he is a jerk, or that he isn't) he will be a jerk. Thomas's point would be that if you define situations accurately (actual, factual, not based on someone else's observation) to begin with, you're a big step ahead in terms of relationship building and avoiding a lot of potential problems.

John Rawls (1922-2002) was a tremendously influential political philosopher whose book, *A Theory of Justice*, has had an enormous impact on people of all academic disciplines and all walks of life throughout many countries. One of Rawls' gems is this question: "Would the best off accept the arrangements if they believed at any moment they might find themselves in the place of the worst off?" He is undoubtedly thinking in broader terms, but the question can aptly apply to the process of building and maintaining relationships on a more personal level. Rawls sounds a lot like Kant and Goethe, and they all sound a lot like the "golden rule": treat others, not as you are treated, but as you would like to be treated. And the other side of this coin is, treat yourself as you want others to treat you. Any genuine attempt at building and maintaining relationships should start with considering what it might be like to be in the place of another person, and another, and another.

One of my favorite stories I discovered in *Cross Currents* magazine (Fall, 1992). There is probably no limit to the ways this story can be interpreted and related to various aspects of life. I think of it in terms of relationship building. The story goes as follows:

Once there was a prince who fell into the delusion of thinking he was a rooster. He took off all his clothes, sat under the table, and refused to eat any food but corn seeds. The king sent for many doctors and many specialists, but none of them could cure him.

Finally a wise man appeared before the king and said: "I think I can cure the prince." The king gave him permission to try.

The wise man took off his clothes, crawled under the table

and began to munch on corn seeds. The prince looked at him suspiciously and said: "Who are you, and what are you doing here?"

The wise man answered: "Who are you, and what are you doing here?"

"I am a rooster," answered the prince belligerently.

"Oh, really? So am I," answered the wise man quietly.

The two of them sat together under the table until they became accustomed to each other. When the wise man felt that the prince was used to his presence, he signaled for some clothing. He put on the clothing and then he said to the prince: "Don't think that roosters can't wear clothing if they want to. A rooster can wear clothes and be a perfectly good rooster just the same."

The prince thought about this for a while, and then he too agreed to put on clothes.

After a time the wise man signaled to have food put under the table. The prince became alarmed and he said: "What are you doing?" The wise man reassured him. "Don't be upset. A rooster can eat the food that human beings eat if he wants to, and still be a good rooster." The prince considered this statement for a time, and then he too signaled for food.

The wise man said to the prince: "Do you think that a rooster has to sit under the table all the time?" A rooster can get up and walk around if he wants to and still be a good rooster." The prince considered these words for a time, and then he followed the wise man up from the table and began to walk.

After he began dressing like a person, eating like a person and walking like a person, he gradually recovered his senses and began to live like a person.

C. Choose Your Friends Carefully

The idea of friendship has held an important place throughout history, especially in the Eastern hemisphere. In some countries friendship is a stronger bond than marriage, and friends can even see themselves as "married." Some Old Testament passages (from Proverbs) offer a glimpse of how strong the friendship bond has been: "A friend loves at all times" (17:17). The implication is that a friend is there in the bad times as well as the good. "There are friends who pretend to be friends, but there is a friend who sticks closer than a brother" (18:24). This verse emphasizes the special quality of friendship. "Make no friendship with a person given to anger" (22:24). The idea is that it would be hard to continually support a person whose frequent anger resulted in bad behavior. "Do not forsake your friend, and your father's friend" (27:10). This represents the strongest aspect of friendship, that real friends never stop being friends.

As a Westerner you probably do not usually take friendship quite so seriously. Nevertheless, you are influenced by the people you associate with, and they by you. There is a lot of truth in the notion that when two individuals encounter each other an exchange takes place. So, you should be careful who you hang around with. You will tend to become like your associates, especially those you consider your closest friends.

An old adage says that birds of a feather flock together. Like many old adages this one is true. Individuals tend to seek out others who are like themselves, who have the same interests, likes and dislikes, background, and so on. No one likes to appear different or to attract unwanted attention. In physics opposites may attract, but not in marriages, friendships or close relationships of any kind. Opposites will only attract trouble. As a general rule likes, in terms of relationships, attract; and you will eventually find others very much like yourself to associate with.

Parents sometimes try to justify a child's bad behavior with the rationale, "Robert was running around with the wrong crowd." The implication is that Robert's behavior was influenced by or caused by the other members of the crowd. This may sound good, and it may be a correct assessment as far as it goes. But it leaves out the fact that Robert was also a willing, participating and contributing member of this crowd, and that he probably influenced the others to about the same degree that they influenced him. Granted, crowds (e.g. gangs) sometimes do things collectively that the individual members may not do by themselves. But blaming the crowd for bad choices and irresponsible behavior misses the point entirely: Namely that, a) friends, associates, crowds/groups are choices, and b) that individuals influence and are influenced by those who make up the group. This is one very good reason why friends and close associates should be chosen carefully, not simply encountered and accepted. Over a period of time, it matters.

An interesting aspect of friendship is that it isn't always easy to distinguish your friends from your enemies. This may not apply with regard to your closest friends, but it does apply generally. There is a story (which has been told in a variety of ways and to make a variety of points) which illustrates this point. A hunter was walking through the woods on a bitterly cold morning when he came upon a half-frozen bird. Feeling sorry for the bird but having no resources in his knapsack with which to deal with the situation, the hunter looked around until he found some freshly deposited, warm manure from an animal that had recently passed by. He quickly gathered up a handful of the manure and packed it around the little bird; then he continued on his way. After a while the warm manure, along with the gradually rising temperature, worked together to provide enough heat to revive the bird which immediately began to sing. A hungry fox prowling nearby heard the bird and promptly went over and ate him.

There are at least three morals to this story. First, those who put you in "it" aren't necessarily your enemies. Second, those who get you out of "it" aren't necessarily your friends. And third, when you're in "it" up to your ears, keep your mouth shut. The point is that your friends may sometimes appears as your enemies, and your enemies may appear as your friends. It is extremely important to understand the difference.

What criteria would you use for choosing a friend? Here are some questions you might want to ask yourself. First, do I like this person? (I have already made a distinction between like and love; love should never be seen as optional; like is optional.) Is this someone I admire and respect? You're not going to be friends for long with someone you find hard to like. There must be a mutual attraction based upon compatibility, common interests, and pursuits or goals. Second, is this someone I can relate to for a long period of time? There is another adage that says "friends are forever." You should choose friends for life, for the long-term, not simply for some immediate purpose. Actually there is no such thing as a short-term friendship. Third, do I "hit it off" with this person? An often used expression is "good chemistry." That is, do you mix well or do you clash often? Is this someone you really enjoy being around, doing things with, conversing with or just spending time with? Or does this person have habits and eccentricities that are annoying to you? Fifth, is this a democratic relationship? Is everything on the level? A Lone Ranger and Tonto kind of relationship may not always work over the long haul. It can be a relationship, but a relationship and a friendship are really two different ships. If one party is subservient to the other, if one party simply uses the other (remember Kant?), or if one party dominates or controls the other in any way (other than the normal exercise of abilities, expertise, and so on) then it probably won't qualify as a friendship. And it probably won't last long, which is a pretty good indication that it wasn't a friendship in the first place.

So, choose your friends carefully, for a true friend is a treasure and hard to come by. A "friend" is trouble and they are everywhere. There will be individuals you will like and some you can't stand. You will have various types of relationships during the course of your lifetime. But you will be lucky and blessed if you have one true friend.

D. Happiness and Self-Esteem

"Don't worry, be happy." These are the lyrics of Billy Crystal's song. It's an old idea that human beings can't seem to come to terms with. It's something everyone wants but cannot agree on what it is and how to get it. Most ethical theories, either directly or indirectly, imply that happiness is something to be sought after. Lynn Peters said, "Happiness isn't about what happens to us, it's about how we perceive what happens to us."

If happiness is your main goal in life, or even a minor one, you will never find it. Happiness should not, in and of itself, be a goal you pursue. Happiness is a by-product of something else; namely, of a life reasonably well lived. Happiness is serendipitous. If you deliberately go looking for it you will probably never find it. If, however, you live a quality lifestyle, take care of yourself and others; in short, if you live by the love principle you will be about as happy as you can be. Nothing else can "make" you happy. Granted, if you live in poverty, poor health and generally miserable surroundings you will be hard pressed to be happy. Nonetheless, the opposite will not automatically create happiness. Happiness is like your shadow; it comes along for the ride. It is always a result of something else.

There are classes for children and adults where self-esteem is taught. Sentiments such as "you are unique," "you are the only person in the whole world like you," and "God made you special" are used to bolster to self-esteem. And physical measures such as new clothing, a new hair style, dental work and simply good grooming and personal hygiene can help "build" self-esteem. All of these things are good. And, like character, integrity and morality self-esteem can be taught to a certain extent. But trying to "feel better" about yourself isn't likely to happen without a reason to feel better.

And there is the problem. The emphasis is not on how you feel; it's on what you do. A young man who makes "A's" and "B's" and is captain of his football team probably doesn't have to worry much about self-esteem. He may have more than he needs. Children can be reminded every day that they are special, unique and loved by God, family and friends. But if they make "D's" and "F's" and see themselves as failures, self-esteem will be low.

An adult who works hard, manages her resources wisely, makes good decisions and involves herself in social and community affairs may not be a genius or rich, but she almost invariably will be reasonably happy and have quite enough self-esteem. While you cannot "just be happy," you can chart a deliberate course of action whereby you will increase the quality of your life and, consequently, you will become a better person. As this happens (and it will happen gradually and methodically) happiness and self-esteem will happen simultaneously. There is simply no other way to do it.

A single, poorly educated mother of three children living in deplorable conditions and without the resources to adequately care for herself and her children can be told all sorts of things by well meaning "friends" trying to help. But until the quality of life for herself and her children changes substantially, self-esteem is a useless term. She must first see herself as a "self" before she can think about self-esteem. Thus, self-esteem like happiness is a by-product of something else. Both come from doing something reasonably well, from a sense of accomplishment. When you are living your life on a level consistent with reasonable expectations self-esteem will be there.

E. Ghosts, Windmills and Dragons

Somewhere several years ago I read something entitled "What are you fighting?" I have no idea where I found this or who wrote it, but I have made a lot of use of it. The author mentioned three types of "battles" which can be labeled as ghosts, windmills and dragons.

Some people fight ghosts. That is, they dwell on the past, recreating and rehearsing bad memories and continually opening old wounds. There isn't a thing that anyone can do to change the past. Yet some people virtually live in the past and constantly think about the past as though it might somehow change to the way they wish it could have been. You may have said, or heard someone say, "Every time I think about thus and so I get mad all over again." The unpleasant event is recreated over and over, like watching a bad movie everyday; or like the movie "Groundhog Day" where the main character is forced to live the same day over and over.

Without doubt you have had experiences which, if you could, you would go back and change. But you can't. The ghosts of the past have to stay in the past. There's no point in trying to fight them because they actually don't exist. They aren't there any longer and they pose no harm or cause for alarm. There is an old adage that says history repeats itself. Actually, history can never repeat itself because time moves on. Similar situations may occur, events may resemble other events, and people can repeatedly make bad decisions, but none of this is the same as history repeating itself. So, if you are waiting for an unpleasant event to happen again you're in for a long wait.

While the past cannot be changed, and there's no point in dwelling on it, you can change the way you think about the past. First, accept the fact that bad things happen to everyone, even to the most fortunate. Second, accept the fact that a lot of good things also happen to everyone, even to the most unfortunate. Third, get the past into perspective. Ghosts don't exist except in the mind. So also it is with the past.

Some people fight windmills. Unlike ghosts, windmills are real but they do not need to be fought with. The idea here is based on the book *Don Quixote* by Miguel de Cervantes (1547-1616). The character of Don Quixote is a strange individual who thinks way beyond his capabilities. He has illusions about being a knight in shining armor. This is an impossible ambition but he imagines himself one anyway. He has a nag for a horse, a homemade, noisy suit of armor and a long pole for a lance. And, to make bad matters worse, he has a vision problem. You get the picture. So, he rides away looking for whatever it is that knights look for. During one of his adventures he sees in the distance what he thinks are giants or monsters. He charges on and attacks them. As it turns out they are windmills. Windmills pose no threat and do not need to be fought with.

The point of this story (for my purposes, at least) should be obvious: Don't get into a battle that doesn't need to be fought. Don't see an enemy if the enemy doesn't exist. And avoid situations that are clearly none of your business. Don't create a problem for yourself. The key is to accurately identify and evaluate the event/situation. We encounter windmills every day (all kinds of situations, potential problem areas); but windmills should be left alone.

What about dragons? Dragons are real. That is, dragons are situations or conditions that pose a threat. They need to be encountered, fought with, and eliminated if possible. Dragons will devour you unless you either kill them or at least keep them at bay (i.e. contain, control). You know exactly what your dragon is. You can name it. A dragon is the thing that keeps you from being the best person you can be. It might be drugs, alcohol, lack of temper control, procrastination, irresponsibility or any number of other things. The good news is that the dragon does not exist that cannot either be killed (eliminated) or defeated (kept in check). When thinking becomes more logical and mature, ghosts will disappear, windmills will not be seen as problems that concern you, and dragons can be completely uprooted out of your life.

F. Get Even or Get Resolved

I was getting out of my car at a shopping center parking lot when I noticed a pickup truck parking next to me. Normally I wouldn't have given it a second thought, but this one caught my attention. It was an average size pickup but it had tremendously oversized tires, giving it the appearance of being much larger. A rifle was conspicuously mounted in the rear window, and on the rear bumper was a sticker that read "I don't get mad, I get even." I waited a few seconds; I was curious. A man approximately thirty-five or so, head shaved, visibly overweight and sporting a T-shirt much too small to cover his protruding belly, jumped down from the cab looking for all the world like a general in search of a war. He looked around, opened the door and took something out, slammed it shut and went around to the back of the truck. He poked around a bit, spat two or three times, and headed toward the main door of the shopping center, all the while glancing back admiringly at his awesome looking truck.

I am relating this story because I want you to see a very insecure man. A secure person does not drive around in a vehicle meant to intimidate. He does not need to affix a weapon across the window for everyone to see and associate with the power and strength of the owner. And he does not need to advertise his insecurity with a bumper sticker that lets everyone know that he is immature, revengeful and lacks good communication skills. A friend of mine said the reason why some people have inferiority complexes is because they are inferior. I'm sure he meant that as a joke. But it's not a joke that insecure individuals often advertise themselves and, thus, exacerbate, their insecurity. Dr. John Smith said, "He that has mastery over his own will feels no violence from without and finds no contest within." Secure individuals have little to fear and nothing to prove. Insecure individuals seem to fear a lot and have a need to prove everything. They find it almost impossible to admit their insecurity for fear that it will cause them to appear all the more insecure. It's a case of a "self-fulfilling prophecy." They want everyone to believe that, instead of getting mad, they take the tougher route of getting even, as though they somehow are beyond mere anger. But, of course they're mad. And they're probably mad much of the time. If they weren't mad they wouldn't try to get even, even to the point of advertising the fact.

Is it actually possible to "get even?" You may choose to retaliate, which is a viable option in certain situations (e.g. national defense) and within reason. Retaliation may have both political and military objectives and consequences, and it may be accomplished legally. But it's not the same as "getting even." Attempting to get even is not a logical option; in fact, it's impossible. You can "react" but your reaction is still an action which you are responsible for. It is possible to think in terms of action, reaction; action, reaction, repeatedly. But it works out in terms of action, another action, followed by yet another action. Nothing in this process gets evened.

Much of the ancient world operated from a religious-politico philosophy called lex talionis (Latin) which means basically an eye for an eye and a tooth for a tooth. It is literally the law of retaliation. In short, it is the reverse of the "golden rule."

As a political philosophy or as a philosophy of life it has never worked very well. It's like trying to operate by the principle of "fight fire with fire." No one would even think of trying to extinguish a fire with a can of gasoline and a blowtorch. Over 2000 years ago Jesus replaced lex talionis with agape, the law of love, and urged others to do the same.

Getting even is not within the realm of possibility. One does not get even, one merely responds to a bad deed with another bad (maybe worse) deed; an action followed by an action. Getting even is impossible because the action begins on uneven ground. The process becomes one of A committing some act, then B going one step ahead by committing another act, then A…It would continue on and on in a never ending, futile, wasteful series of actions where strategy eventually would become meaningless. If it were possible to get even, it would be possible to stay even, which of course, would terminate the process. Arbitration or litigation is sometimes a necessary and only rational way to settle disputes. Otherwise, trying by your own devices to hurt another person who has hurt you is not only futile, it is morally reprehensible. Not only that, revenge is self-destructive. The revenge-er inflicts a self-wound as bad or worse than the revenge-ee.

G. Issue vs. Personality

In a conflict situation there's going to be disagreement. That's what conflict is. And sometimes in the course of dealing with a conflict parties may tend to become confused between the issue at hand and the personalities involved. That is, they may lose sight of the real issue and began focusing on personalities (on each other). Whenever a battle of personalities ensues it becomes impossible to declare a winner or to reach an agreeable solution to the problem. Any effort toward a solution must begin with trying to define and clarify the issue, and sort out any related issues. Usually in a conflict situation there is one major issue. The objective, then, is to define the issue and deal with it. Separate personalities from issues. You are not likely to have either the time or the skills necessary to try to change personalities. And when a personality becomes the issue there is little hope of a successful resolution.

One way of dealing with the issue rather than the personality is to never take someone's negative remarks personally. This isn't always easy to do, and it takes understanding, skill, patience and a certain level of maturity. Sometimes the things people say are out of the desperation of being at their wits end, out of the embarrassment of the moment, or of not knowing precisely or properly how to handle a particular situation. Everyone is bound to do or say something terribly stupid occasionally. So, rather than always taking offense, give the other person some room. Allow her to bow out gracefully if possible. And always leave an escape route for her as well as for yourself. If you learn to identify and deal with what the issue really is, you will discover that in many instances it isn't all that important.

H. Crisis or Interruption?

Jerry sat in a counseling group in a correctional institution. It was his turn to present an "negative event evaluation" (i.e. relate something that happened which he did not handle very well, and which he was willing to examine and discuss with the other members of the group). He served five years on his sentence and was granted parole less than six months earlier. While living at home Jerry worked, saved some money and with a little help from his mother he did something he had dreamed of since he was a little boy. He made a down payment on a new Corvette. A few days after he purchased the car he drove to the mall. As he was walking toward the mall entrance he heard a sound, and he turned around just in time to see the car that had backed into his car driving out of the parking lot. Jerry quickly jumped back into his car and followed what appeared to be an elderly lady for six or seven miles. Apparently she wasn't aware she had backed her car into his. When she turned into her driveway Jerry was right behind her. When she reached the front door of her house Jerry grabbed her by her shoulder, pushed her against the door and threatened to kill her. A next door neighbor standing in his yard rushed over to intervene.

Jerry was returned to prison, his parole was revoked, and he faced a new charge of assault. As he reconstructed his evaluation of the event (i.e. what he was thinking at the time his car was hit and when he was threatening the elderly lady) these are the actual sentences he wrote on the board:

1. I can't believe she hit my car.
2. The damned old bitch can't drive.
3. I'm going to kill her.
4. Old people shouldn't be allowed to have a drivers' license.

The group discussion centered on whether the statements were logical/rational or illogical/irrational and why. As we examined each statement closely it became apparent that they were not logical or provable, nor did they reflect a very high level of maturity. There were glaring flaws with each statement. Jerry tried to defend his statements but they wouldn't hold up under close scrutiny. The only statement that even had the appearance of being logical was number four which was his opinion, and even it was mean spirited.

Look at the first sentence. Why can't he believe it? He was looking at the dent in the door. How could he deny it? He must have believed the lady hit his car unless he wanted to lie to himself and/or deny reality. There is nothing logical about the statement. And the same with the second. The lady wasn't damned. This was merely his own use of frustration language, and he didn't have the power or authority to damn her. His observation that she was a female dog is so incorrect as to not even merit comment.(This was, of course, discussed in the group.) His remark that the lady couldn't drive was proven inaccurate by his earlier statement that he followed her for six or seven miles. He observed her driving, so it made little sense to say she couldn't drive. Sentence three is grossly absurd. How could he even think of killing someone over an incident as small and insignificant as a dented car door! Such blatant irrationality is difficult to comprehend. The last statement is his opinion which he was entitled to, but which appeared to be tainted with unjustified prejudice due to his anger, causing it to also be irrational and unreasonable.

This incident illustrates what can happen when an event is evaluated irrationally. Jerry's faulty thinking led to inappropriate emotions (i.e. anger and wanting revenge), and to inappropriate actions (i.e. harassing and threatening to kill the elderly lady). It also illustrates how a problem can be evaluated as a crisis instead of an interruption. Dented fenders are a common occurrence. Granted what occurred was an aggravation, something one would rather not have to be bothered with. Such things do happen occasionally, but such events are not crises. The situation could have been dealt with effectively and rationally by calling the police, his insurance agent and someone to pick him up at the mall if necessary. The root of the problem, as always, was with the thinking process. Jerry evaluated the event totally out of proportion to the event itself. The event, his evaluation of the event, his choice of emotion and his choice of action were not on the same level. The event was probably a level II and he dealt with it as a level IV.

I. Why vs. What and How

David, a ten year old known for his tempter tantrums, was a resident at a home for children where I worked. When he tried to hit another child with a baseball he missed his target but shattered a window. He was brought to me for "counseling." Now, I could have said, "David, why did you do this?" And I would have gotten a good excuse. He would have answered my question with something like "I was mad at Billy because he did something to me" (i.e. I was a victim seeking justice). Then I could have said "David, how does it make you feel knowing that you did something wrong?" And I'll grant you that he would have been woefully sorry for his "mistake," and he would have told me so. Then I could have sent him to his room to reflect on what he had done, and we would dialogue about it later when he felt better.

I didn't take that course of action. Actually, my brief conversation with David went something like this:

JS: Hi, David; what's going on?

D: I accidentally broke a window in Ms. Smith's cottage.

JS: Really? How did that happen?

D: I threw a baseball and it went too far.

JS: I see. Well, accident or not, what are you going to do about it? How are you planning to straighten this out?

This conversation went on for a few more minutes. I asked "what" and "how" questions and David gradually formulated a plan to clean up his mess. The necessary steps were to first apologize to Ms. Smith for causing the problem, sweep up the glass so no one would step on it, ask the maintenance person to help him replace the window, and pay for the cost from his allowance (which also meant that he couldn't go to the movie on Friday night because he didn't have enough money, and I wouldn't allow him to borrow some). Not once did I ask David why he did what he did or how he felt about anything. It really didn't matter how he felt. He had to take responsibility for his irresponsible action. He had to do something, not talk about how he felt. Once he began a definite course of positive action his emotions would change anyway.

The point: Trying to determine how you feel doesn't clean up the mess. It doesn't repair, mend or fix. You feel as you think, as you choose to feel. Asking "why" questions only results in excuse making, and as long as you have an excuse you will never get your problem solved. Ask yourself, what do I need to do in this particular circumstance? Formulate a simple but inclusive plan to get it done, and start working on it. By the time you are finished your thinking will have changed for the better. And, by the way, knowing that you have logically, ethically, maturely and successfully dealt with a problem brings its own degree of therapy.

J. Tact: Ms. Miller's Method

Undoubtedly there are times and circumstances when the load-aim-fire approach may be the only way to deal with conflict, but not always. And the straight-off-the shoulder approach may work if all else seems to fail, but often all else has not been given an opportunity. Diplomacy (on a more formal level) and tact (on a more personal level) will usually prove to be the best course of action in conflict situations or tense moments. Tact is a word with both French and Latin roots and it refers to sense of touch, or simply to touch. Using tact is having a keen sense of what to do or say to keep good relations with others.

One of my college ethics professors told how his wife used tact in sensitive situations, but she was also determined to always be truthful. And that can be a delicate balancing act. It may be difficult to be tactful and truthful at the same time.

Ms. Miller had a method that worked well for her. On one occasion, which happened to be Sunday morning, a young woman brought her recently born baby to church for the first time. When she saw Ms. Miller she exclaimed with prideful excitement, "Don't you think she's just the most beautiful baby you've ever seen in your entire life!?" Well, that may have presented a dilemma for some: telling the truth regardless or saying something that would appear unkind. But for Ms. Miller handling such superlatives was no problem. In typical fashion she took the baby in her arms and, with a big smile replied so that everyone around could hear, "Oh, my! Now that is a baby!" Actually Ms. Miller didn't really think that was the most beautiful baby she had ever seen. Not even close. (She probably reserved that description for her own children.) It was pure and precious, but pudgy and puckered. But Ms. Miller knew how to "have her cake and eat it too." She wanted to avoid offending the young mother, and she also wanted to avoid telling an outright lie. So, she used tact. Her statement sounded for all the world like a nice compliment about the baby. And it was taken as a compliment. But it was also a truthful statement. That was, indeed, a baby. It was the way she said it that made all the difference.

Consider another example: A husband and wife are about to go out for dinner and a movie. The wife asks, "Honey, do you think this new dress looks good on me?" The husband turns around to see what he immediately thinks is probably the most awful looking dress he has ever seen. That's what he actually thinks. So, how does he respond? Does he stick to the truth and tell her exactly what he thinks and possibly ruin what would otherwise be a pleasant evening? Not if he's smart. He can satisfy her desire to believe she looks good in the dress, and his wanting to avoid telling a lie. Tactfully, he says, "Wow! I'll bet you really like that dress!" It sounds like a compliment, and his wife is happy. And it is, in fact, a dress. And of course she likes it or she wouldn't have bought it. Again, it was the way it was said rather than what was said that made the difference between an unnecessary and hurtful blunder and getting on with the occasion.

The ethics of the "little white lie" can be debated endlessly, but for me there's no debate. A so called white lie isn't really a lie. A lie is a deliberate, deceitful distortion of the truth without regard for consequences. Immanuel Kant thought that a lie was the worst thing a person could do because it damages integrity. If you tell a lie, a deliberate untruth, knowingly and irresponsibly, you may not be believed even when you tell the truth. It's the idea of not knowing for sure whether what is said is true or not that poses the biggest problem. On the other hand, a white lie is an attempt to be tactful and gracious, to withhold certain thoughts or information that isn't necessary and which could exacerbate a situation unnecessarily. It's important to understand the difference and to not make a big deal of always telling "the truth" regardless. There may be times when the hard truth can be much worse than a white lie. The key is to be discriminating and reasonable. Truth and tact are not mutually exclusive.

K. Perspective Has A Vanishing Point

Perspective is viewing things (objects, events) in their relationship or importance to other things. In paintings/ photos objects are represented as having depth and distance. Thus, perspective reflects realness in relation. Medieval art, for example, lacked perspective. Objects that should appear as distant, and therefore smaller, instead appear as large as the closest objects, presenting a distorted image instead of a real life-like image.

An interesting aspect of perspective as it relates to paintings/pictures is that it has a vanishing point. All paintings that are realistic (i.e. not surrealistic, or some forms of modern art) have a vanishing point, a point at which it appears all lines converge and end. An excellent example is the painting of the Last Supper. All lines lead to Christ (or more accurately to the head of Christ) which, in this painting, is the vanishing point. In other paintings it isn't quite as simple to determine where the vanishing point is located but its there. It is a point in the painting where it appears that everything comes together with nowhere else to go. The idea that there is anything more to see simply "vanishes." When you see the painting/picture, that's all there is.

The notion of perspective as a vanishing point has therapeutic as well as aesthetic value. One of the problems with E2 (evaluation, the process of making determinations, judgments, decisions about E1, event) is that a particular event may not be viewed in proper perspective. Either too much emphasis and/or value is given to one or more aspects of the event, or, by the same token, too little; too much here and too little there without achieving a balanced, nuanced viewpoint. That is, events can be perceived and evaluated out of perspective. Things that should be "up front" aren't given much value, and things that should appear in the distance and small are given an importance out of proportion to their real value, and the result looks like a medieval painting.

When an event is seen in perspective (i.e. in context with surrounding circumstances and in regard to its relative importance) it may be said to have a vanishing point. If the event is evaluated accurately, without prejudice, then there is nothing else to add or subtract. It is simply what it is. Events can range from practically insignificant to highly significant, and the evaluation process should be the same. Perspective may require little or no call for action, or it may require immediate, drastic action depending on how the event is evaluated and the significance attached to it. In any case perspective should create a vanishing point which helps eliminate the possibility for irrational emotion and irrational action. There's nothing left to do except leave it alone and move on. All other roads to further irrational speculation are closed. Perspective involves the whole picture, understanding the larger context.

Baruch (or Benedict de) Spinoza (Dutch philosopher, 1632-1677) adds an important dimension to perspective. Basically he said that it is absurd for you to be obsessed by your personal problems. You should try to see your problems as occupying the place they actually do in the totality of things. Then you shall see certain problems as insignificant, and you will be better able to bear them. (Franklin Roosevelt said that the problems he faced seemed much smaller while taking a walk on a starlit night.) Three of Spinoza's major concepts are balance, toleration and perspective. The point is, many of our problems will vanish when we see them in perspective and in the totality of things. The idea is in the statement "I felt sorry for myself because I had no shoes until I saw a man with no feet." Perspective is powerful, and powerfully enlightening.

L. Can't Forget, Can Forgive

You've heard it many times: "Forgive and forget." Like many adages and advice it's only half true. You can't forget, and there's no reason why you should. The things that happen (events) during the course of your life are part of your total experience and, therefore, part of your memory. You forget a lot of things of course because they are so routine and trivial and hardly worth remembering. Sometimes you wish you could remember things you can't. But you do usually remember the most important things along with other things you simply can't seem to forget.

You can forgive, and you should forgive. There are at least two aspects of forgiveness that should be understood, otherwise trying to forgive may become an exercise in frustration: absorption and deflection. The American Civil

War began when Union troops began firing on Fort Sumter at Charleston, South Carolina on April 12, 1861. They started around 4:30 p.m. and the ordeal lasted much longer than anyone could have imagined. The fort took a tremendous pounding before finally falling. The reason it took so long to bring Sumter down was because the original fort (unlike the brick and concrete there today) was built of palmetto trees, a type of soft pine with the ability to absorb the impact of the heavy cannon balls. As the wooden walls of Fort Sumter absorbed the impact of the attack it simultaneously deflected much of the cannon artillery.

The firing on Fort Sumter is a picture of forgiveness, absorption and deflection. When things happen that are interpreted as bad, hurtful, unfair or awful the first thing you may want to do is "get even" or retaliate. Bad things do happen. And whatever happens cannot be changed or undone. It becomes part of your experience; it cannot simply go away. You cannot ignore the reality of your experience and you shouldn't try to. In other words, you can't forget. You're stuck with the experience of events and your memory of them. You must absorb some or many of the blows. Absorption hurts. If someone hits you in the stomach with a fist (or a barrage of negative verbiage) you feel it. And you may say that it's unfair, it shouldn't have happened, and so on.

The other side of the coin of forgiveness is that while absorption is happening, deflection is also at work. Deflection is simply realizing that much of the artillery that assails you on a daily basis doesn't matter much. A lot of the shots being fired are from pea shooters instead of cannons. They inflict no real damage or actual pain. Intent and insult may be there, and it may not be very pleasant, but this is where perspective comes into play. Once the "attack" is viewed as it really is: mean, intentional, hurtful, unfair, that's it. There's no more in the picture; there's nowhere else to go with it. Forgiveness is the only logical, mature response.

What else can you do with people but love them? What else can you do in the face of hurt and injustice (at least that makes any sense) than forgive? Granted, there may be situations that call for more direct, drastic measures, such as litigation. But even so, forgiveness should not be viewed as incompatible with justice.

Forgiveness is necessary both for you as well as for the perpetrator of the evil. To the perpetrator you are saying: Yes, what you did was hateful, hurtful and unjust; but I refuse to allow your actions to interfere with my plans or to define who I am now or ever. That is, I will not go through life known as the man who was wronged by Martin. Furthermore, I recognize the act you committed for what it was, but I release you from any ill will, threats or retaliation from me. And I will not carry around the unnecessary baggage of hate, resentment and the wish to "get even." So, there; for my part, it's over. I have this all in perspective and perspective has a vanishing point.

M. You Can't/Can Be Perfect

If I could eliminate certain words from the English language as easily as striking the delete key on the computer keyboard, the word "perfect" would almost certainly be among the dozen or so I would eliminate. Although it is a commonly used word, it is virtually meaningless because it practically defies definition. Most often perfect is used within a context of making excuses for ones behavior or for putting someone in their place. For example, "I'm not perfect, you know," or "you must think you're perfect" (meaning you're not). Most dictionaries define perfect or perfection in terms of being without fault or defect, or a high state of excellence. In counseling groups when someone uses the term "perfect" I usually ask her what she means. After a variety of responses are given everyone finally realizes that it's a tricky word.

One of the best known, but perhaps most contested, of Plato's philosophical doctrines is his theory of forms. Simply, Plato argues that while there is not a perfect anything to be found on earth, somewhere there is an ideal form of each thing. You may draw a really round circle or make a very square box, but the circle isn't perfectly round and the box isn't perfectly square. There's a flaw somewhere regardless of how minute. But ideally there exists a perfect circle and a perfect square. This is a way of trying to make sense of Plato's idea of perfection; that perfect things exist only in the mind.

On the one hand (and from a more practical standpoint) forget about perfection. If your goal in life is to become a perfect person, not only will you fall immeasurably short, you will be trying to attain a goal you probably cannot even adequately define. And, by the same token, if you are expecting perfection from your spouse, your children or your employees, the same thinking applies. Neither you, nor they, are going to become perfect, given the usual understanding of the term as flawless or without error.

On the other hand you can be perfect, but you need to change the way you think about it. Perfection actually is possible if you delete "perfect" and insert "complete." Imagine a basketball player taking a fifteen foot shot and the ball swishing through the net, never touching the rim. Someone is likely to exclaim, "That was a perfect shot." And it was perfect. The scoreboard reflects an increase of three points. Now again imagine that same player a few minutes later taking another fifteen foot shot from nearly the same spot. But this time the ball hits one side of the rim, bounces high and comes down on the other side of the rim, rolls around and stands still for half a second while the crowd gasps, and it finally falls thought the net. An announcer might comment on what an ugly shot that was, and she would be right from the standpoint of form and execution. But basketball games are not won on such criteria as pretty or ugly. They are won on how many times the ball goes through the hoop within the allotted time frame. In this instance the ball went through the net. The scoreboard increased by three points. In that sense, the second shot was as perfect as the first.

In the New Testament the word perfect means mature, and it also means to complete. Defined in this way it is possible to be perfect. Telling yourself that you are not perfect may be an excuse for not doing some things you need to do. If you complete what you set out to accomplish, you are, at least at that point, perfect. If you are making progress toward your objectives, you are becoming perfect. Being first and being perfect is not the same. Don't fall into the habit of seeing yourself in competition with someone else, or of pacing yourself according to another person's agenda. Granted, only one individual wins a race, but others may finish (complete) the race also. And besides, life really isn't a race; it's a pace, a journey. The upshot of the matter is, if you want to be perfect (i.e. to complete what you set out to do) proceed at your own pace and according to your own agenda. Also, you need to keep your goals practical and achievable. You can never be perfect if you think of perfection as trying to achieve some pie-in-the-sky, impossible-to-define goal. But you can if you complete your clearly defined objectives deliberately, constantly, daily. Then the statement of Jesus in the "Sermon on the Mount" (Matthew 5:48) will not seem like such an impossible task: "You, therefore, must be perfect, as your heavenly Father is perfect."

The idea of non-perfection should never become an excuse for unethical actions. Dr. David H.C. Read said, "Nobody's perfect" has become the slogan of the cynics who have ceased to take seriously any moral standard whatever. Nobody's perfect; therefore, anything goes." But we can't get by with that kind of thinking anymore. Anyone who makes the effort can be perfect. That places a tremendous amount of responsibility on each individual, doesn't it?

N. You Had Better Sweat the Small Stuff

The book *Don't Sweat the Small Stuff* was a great success and a good book because the author made some excellent points. But I want to approach the notion of small stuff from the opposite angle. It's true that a lot of small stuff is not worth a drop of sweat. However, as a general principle, the importance of small stuff cannot be overemphasized. It's a huge mistake to assume that because something is small that it isn't important. Little things may not be little; they may only appear to be little. The relationship between size and importance or function can be easily underestimated. M. A. Kelty said, "Watch your way…as a cautious traveler; and don't be gazing at that mountain or river in the distance and saying, 'how shall I ever get over them?' But keep to the present little inch that is before you, and accomplish that in the moment that belongs to it." It's the "little inch" that, so often in the business of daily living, can be "the rub." Doing the little things, and at the precise moment, are the basic ingredients of any successes you are going to have.

I read somewhere that Vince Lombardi was a successful football coach primarily because he worked from a single, simple strategy: get the first down. It was allegedly this idea that won the Super Bowl championship for the Green Bay Packers more than once. The completed long pass is a huge yard gainer, and it's exciting for both players and fans. But probably more long passes are failures than successes. Big stuff can be very risky if it doesn't work out. If the primary goal of a football game is to win, what's the best strategy? Supposedly, with Coach Lombardi the goal of every play was to move the ball forward at least four or five yards. So you design plays with a high percentage of going that short distance; and you practice until you can execute the plays with skill and confidence. It takes ten yards for a first down. And a series of first-downs results in a touchdown. With a strong defense and a high percentage offense the chance of winning a lot of football games is increased. The important concept is the “little inch,” or with Lombardi, a few yards at a time.

I once attended a conference where an executive with the Prudential Insurance Company was the keynote speaker. He began by asking why are some insurance agents successful while others are not? For example, given two individuals about the same age and with similar backgrounds, why would one be successful and the other a failure? He said only about one out of fifteen agents became successful and stayed with the company. I expected to hear some really spectacular piece of information, some little piece of wisdom that I had apparently missed along the way. What the speaker said was spectacular but, after a moments reflection, not surprising. He said the difference between the two agents is that one is willing to do those little, often unpleasant or distasteful things that the other isn’t willing to do: staying a little longer at the office on Monday instead of rushing home to watch football on T.V.; making a few more calls resulting in a few more appointments, a few more sales and better paychecks. This extra effort, though appearing small, ultimately and over time can pay tremendous dividends.

Research was done involving the police departments of two major cities with two different philosophies of dealing with crime. One department operated by the principle of dealing with the big stuff. That is, police officers have better things to do than issue citations for jaywalking, throwing trash on the streets and speeding five or ten miles over the limit. The result was that overall crime increased remarkably over a period of time. The operating philosophy of the police department of the other city was quite the opposite. Officers were told to deal with each and every violation of the law they witnessed. They were not to ignore anything. In other words, take care of the small stuff. Over the period of time the study involved, the overall crime rate went down. Not only minor infractions but major crime decreased as well. An obvious conclusion of the study was that it pays to take care of the little things. The broader conclusion might be that if the seemingly small stuff is dealt with the big stuff will be less existent or at least easier to manage.

There are many other examples of how important little things, small amounts, a fraction of a second can be in the difference between success or failure, triumph or tragedy. Adding a fraction of a percent on the interest on your loan or your savings account can make a staggering difference over a period of time. Studies show that children who exercise in the classroom daily by simply jumping up and down for a couple of minutes at the end of each hour lose weight and are in better health at the end of the school year than children who do not practice this little routine. There's no question that you shouldn't sweat some small stuff. And it's important to know which small stuff not to sweat. However, as a principle to live by, if you don't take care of the so-called small stuff on a daily, consistent basis, it can become big stuff in a hurry. It's those little, often aggravating, unpleasant, unexciting, mundane things that we would rather not have to put up with that tend to make all the difference in the overall quality of life. Taking care of the business at hand, that's sweating the small stuff.

O. Twenty-Five Percent Isn't Bad

Jesus told the parable of the sower who went out to sow seeds. Some seeds fell along the path and were eaten by birds. Others fell on rocky ground where there was little soil and they couldn't take root. Still other seeds fell among the weeds where they were choked out. But some fell on good soil where they produced abundantly. What is the point of the story? Actually, there may be several lessons, but the main idea is that seventy-five percent of the work the sower did was to no avail. Only twenty-five percent of the seeds grew. I think the overriding point is that you need to learn to live with small gains. It isn't always possible for every seed you plant to grow. When Walgreen started what became the largest drug store chain in the country he learned early on that every store he built wasn't going to be a success. In fact, it's interesting that only about one out of four became successes. Of course, he didn't know which ones would or would not become successful. But the ones that were successful more than made up for the failures, allowing the business to grow. In Jesus' parable the seeds that grew more than made up for those that didn't. You need to keep in mind that everything you do isn't going to work out like you thought. There will be setbacks. Some endeavors are bound to fail. But if you can capitalize on your successes your overall plan will likely be successful. Work with the idea that it is the successes, and often little successes, that negate whatever failures occur. The little gains are often the only ones you have, but they are all you need.

P. You Never Know What You Might Do, Or, Do You?

Regardless of motives or methods, incidents (events) often have dubious results. When someone handles a situation differently than the way you might have expected, or different from the way you think you might have handled it, you may be inclined to say: Well, you never know what you might do in such and such a situation. During job interviews you may have been asked how you would deal with a certain hypothetical situation. And all you can do at that moment is quickly construct a response to match the imaginary situation. The fact is, you may not know what you would do in certain situations, especially if you have never been faced with that particular situation previously.

There is no way of knowing exactly what you or anyone else is likely to do in specific events. It's the word "exactly" that's the problem. Exactly is hard to define in ordinary language. However, you had better have a pretty good idea what you would do in most situations. And, perhaps more importantly, what you would not do. In other words, you should learn to think and act within a framework, a set of boundaries, with which you are very familiar and outside of which you are almost certain you will not venture. Granted, situations (events), and your behavior, cannot be predicted or anticipated with absolute certainty. But you need to know yourself with a high degree of probability. That is, you should know your own values and perimeters, your strengths and vulnerabilities well enough to know how you are likely to behave if and when certain events occur. If you don't have at least a reasonably good idea, there's no telling what you are likely to do. You would be dangerously unpredictable not only to yourself but also to others as well. To put it another way, you would lack one of the most important virtues discussed and emphasized by philosophers from Socrates (Plato), the Stoics and down to the present: self control.

An inmate in a counseling group related the incident that brought him to the correctional institution. He had an excruciating headache and his boss gave him permission to leave work a couple of hours early. He got home around 2:00 p.m. instead of the usual 4:00 p.m. where, much to his surprise, he discovered his wife in bed with a man. He immediately picked up his rifle from behind the door and shot the man, then tried to shoot his wife who escaped through the window and ran down the street. To shorten this story to its obvious conclusion, here sat this man facing several years in prison for murder and attempted murder. After some discussion another member of the group asked him why he chose to handle the situation the way he did. After failing to come to grips with the matter he finally said, "You just never know what you might do."

This statement is true if it refers to details, but it isn't necessarily true in terms of principle. It doesn't take into account what you would not do, or at least what you are not likely to do. For example, I could say that I do not know exactly what I would do if I encounterd the same situation. There would certainly be some decisions to make both immediately and later. And the relationship would unquestionably be seriously compromised. But I can say truthfully, and with a high degree of certainty (probably 99 percent) that in that particular situation I would not shoot anyone. There are many options that can be taken in such a situation just as there are any number of courses of action that can immediately be ruled out.

While you may not know exactly, in detail, what you would do in a particular situation, or how you would do it, you should have a pretty good idea of the boundaries, the perimeters within which you would act. You don't have to be able to predict the future in order to know yourself, your beliefs and values, your view of yourself and others; in short, your philosophy of life, well enough to know that regardless of what happens you will make the best decisions possible; rational, mature decisions you can live with.

The philosopher Emmanuel Kant provides some insight into the ethics of decision making. In his *Critique of Pure Reason* (1781) he gives his famous categorical imperative: "There is...only a single categorical imperative and it is this: Act only on that maxim through which you can at the same time will that it should become a universal law." In more simple language, what would be the result if everyone imitated your actions? For example: You are driving down the street eating a bar of candy and you throw the wrapper out of the window. On first thought it isn't such a bad thing. It's littering, but only a little; a minor offense at worst. But, then what if every driver in the country threw out a candy wrapper (or something similar) at the same time you did? What would be the result? Now the picture changes considerably. Instead of a single piece of litter on the street there would be a ton or tons. So, when viewed in the larger perspective, the decision to toss out the candy wrapper was probably not a good idea. Kant would say that if you decide that your action should not be copied by everyone, then you have an obligation, a duty, to not do it yourself.

Some would say that Kant's categorical imperative is simply a dressed up version of the "golden rule" which states "Do to others as you would have them do to you" (Luke 6:31 NRSV). This "imperative" of Jesus has been stated in various ways in religious teaching throughout the world. And the message is quite clear: Treat others like you want to be treated (assuming, of course, that you want to treat yourself well). This practically universal "rule" could be considered the basic element of all ethical doctrine. It is actually another way of talking about the love principle. That is, you should always (from a sense of duty) act in the best interest of others, and also in your own best interest, insofar as you understand what that interest is. With the categorical imperative or the golden rule as a guiding principle it shouldn't be too difficult to know with a high degree of certainty what you will and will not do in most situations. If the man in prison for murder had acted in accordance with what seemed good for everyone concerned (including himself), his marriage may or may not have survived, but most likely he would not have been serving a prison sentence. You can, in fact, know what you are likely to do in almost every situation. It's all in the way you think.

SUMMARY

A. PROBLEMS

I have organized the contents of this book under four major sections: problems, solutions, change, and applications. As examples of some problem areas, I discuss the importance of language and how the wrong use of language is at the root of many problems that may come to be called "emotional" or "behavioral" problems; the notion of therapy and how therapy so often focuses on feelings and behavior rather than on thinking; the terms "mental health" and "mental illness" which I believe are the wrong terms to describe what might best be described as logical, rational, mature thinking as opposed to faulty, irrational, immature thinking; and the generic use of the term "emotion(al)" which is basically useless because it is non-descriptive and unspecific.

B. SOLUTIONS

If these are problem areas (and there are certainly more than four problem areas; I have selected only what I consider major ones), then what are possible solutions? Obviously there may be more than one method of dealing with the problems. However, I have focused on what I have come to call Event Evaluation Training (or E.E.T. Sometimes I use training and therapy interchangeably) as a vehicle for discovering some solutions. The main idea is that when thinking changes, emotions and actions change accordingly (i.e. will be more appropriate).Thus, if the thinking process is logical, clear, and on a mature level, then whatever emotions that follow will be on the same level. And, consequently, actions (behavior) will be on the same level: namely, more civil, less hurtful and destructive, and more in line with accepted social standards and high ethical and personal expectations. Of course, just the opposite can also occur. Illogical, muddy, immature thinking will result in emotions and behavior that are on the same level with such thinking.

An important component of the solutions section is what I call the T.E.A. formula. And it is always in that order: Thinking-Emotion-Action. Thinking produces emotion(s), followed by action(s). Of course, emotion may or may not play a large part in the choice of actions. The place of emotion should never be discounted, but its influence on behavior may be anywhere on a continuum from virtually nil to extremely evident.

Another important component of the solutions section, actually the "heart" of the E.E.T. program, is the "E" formula: Event (E1), Evaluation (E2), and Emotion (E3). Event is whatever is happening on a minute by minute, hour by hour, day by day basis. It is simply the process of living your life, whatever and however that may be. Evaluation is the idea that you constantly evaluate/interpret and make judgments about whatever is happening. You can do that anywhere between not very well and very well. The quality of your evaluation will determine the appropriateness of your emotion(s) and your resultant action(s) (behavior). Emotion (a difficult concept to come to terms with) is basically a physical manifestation of the thinking process, usually referred to as the way you feel. There is a fourth "E" (Effect, E4) or what finally results from the previous three "E's." The key to the "E" formula is this: E1 does not cause or produce E3; in fact, E2 causes or produces E3. If you do not understand and put into practice this key, you have missed the most important point of the book.

C. CHANGE

The section on change includes twelve topics designed to emphasize the idea that while real, genuine change is difficult, not only is change possible, it is essential in order for the quality of life to improve. And it is important to realize that real, life-enhancing change is based upon a decision to change and the resolve to stay with the process. There are no gimmicks, short-cuts or magical interventions. Religious faith (and the various components of faith: prayer, study of scripture, corporate worship, community service) is extremely important. However, you are ultimately responsible for your behavior.

D. APPLICATIONS

This section is designed to help you put into practice what you have (hopefully) learned from reading this book and contemplating/reflecting on the ideas presented. The sixteen topics deal with some of the most common issues individuals are faced with on a daily basis: love, relationships and friendship, self-esteem, holding grudges vs. forgiveness, tact, the importance of "small stuff," perseverance, capitalizing on small gains, making ethical decisions, and so on. Group participants have asked a lot of interesting questions and contributed engagingly and creatively to the various topics.

Made in the USA
Monee, IL
08 November 2026

67380508R00096